MONEY, GOD & YOU

How It Really Works!

SERAH LISTER

Serah Lister

LEGAL DISCLAIMER

© Serah Lister

ISBN 978-0-9929137-1-7

The moral right of the author has been asserted.

Apart from any fair dealing for the purposes of research or private study; or criticism or review, as permitted under the copyright, Designs and Patents Act 1988,
this publication may only be reproduced, stored or transmitted, in any form or by any means, with prior permission in writing of the publishers, or in the case of reprographic reproduction in accordance with the terms of the licenses issued by the Copyright Licensing Agency.
Enquiries concerning reproduction outside those terms should be sent to the publisher.

Email: serah@serahlister.com

Publisher address:
Kianjirigua Publishing,
44a Croydon Road,
London, SE20 7AE
United Kingdom

DEDICATION

To my son Andrew, I waited for 8 years to see and hold you in my arms. You don't belong to me but to Him who sent you here; you chose me among others to be your guardian for a time and I am forever grateful!

I exhort you to revere and be centred in Elohim; the great I AM, your source, the light of your life.

I love you beyond words! Never stop seeking after the truth for truth brings freedom.

Serah Lister

TABLE OF CONTENTS

Introduction 09

CHAPTER 1. I WILL BLESS YOU 13
   Who Cares? 13
   My Pain and Struggles 15

CHAPTER 2. BIBLICAL PROSPERITY 21
   His Will 21
   Is Prosperity From God? 24
   Poverty is a curse! 29
   We've been redeemed from the Curse 35
   Stop the Money and Mammon Talk 36

CHAPTER 3. BIBLICAL HALL OF WEALTH 43
   Flaunt It! 43
   Job 45
   Abraham 50
   David 54
   Jacob 60

CHAPTER 4. PROSPERITY PRINCIPLES 65
   It's A Deal! 65
   Giving and Receiving 71
   Tithing or Tenth (10%) 77
   Plant Good Seeds 85

CHAPTER 5. THE HUMAN OPERATING SYSTEM™ (hOS™) 91
   Beliefs 91
   Culture 97
   Religion 101
   Education 105
   Rebirth 111

CHAPTER 6. RESPECT THE BUSINESS OF GOD 115
   Jehovah Jireh 115
   True Humility and Defeating Fear 119
   Become A Money Magnet 124
   Generosity versus Greed 128

CHAPTER 7. THE FRUITS OF LAW AND GRACE 133

Justified 133
Religiosity! 136
Bondage or Freedom 141
Scarcity or Abundance 145
Judgment or Forgiveness 149

CHAPTER 8. ASK, SEEK, KNOCK AND IT IS GIVEN 153
Ask 153
Negativity 158
Spiritual Persona 161
Press On 165
Trauma to Transformation 169
FINAL WORDS 171

BONUS CONTENT 172

FAITH – THE EDGE OF BELIEVE! 172

'20 BEAUTIFUL WOMEN –AFRICA EDITION' 176

Acknowledgments

To Florence Kioko, you took a chance on our friendship and invited me a to a youth camp many years ago, and my life has never been the same!

Muthoni, you never judged me; your unconditional love spoke of a love greater than anything I had ever experienced and has shaped my ministry to others.

Andrew Lister, you are my number one teacher and many times you remind me that God is not an angry old man up in the sky. Your depth of understanding the mysteries of God confirm the words of Jesus in Matthew 11:25 – *'You have hidden these things from the wise and learned, and revealed them to little children'*.

My Mastermind (SLM), Janet Blair and Naomi Soko, I am so blessed to have you in my life; you keep me accountable! Remembering Hollywood, all things work together for good.

Kenneth Hagin, though we never met you taught me the foundations of faith, freedom from sickness and poverty.

Bishop Kitonga, my deepest gratitude to you for having faith in a stranger.

To my late friend and brother John Kibe, priceless and gone home early. Remember those long Saturdays working the streets of Nairobi tirelessly to make a difference to the destitute children!

Youth With A Mission (YWAM) Holmsted Manor January and May 1996 DTS, you gave me wings to manifest my faith on another level!

There is no pearl without the oyster and I would like to thank pastors who allowed me to serve in their ministry over the years.

Finally, to my father, the man who never treated me like a girl, set high expectations on my achievements so I could be the woman I am today. I LOVE YOU eternally!

INTRODUCTION

Over the last 20 years living in the United Kingdom, I have seen God move in what can only be described as miraculous; way beyond my comprehension. I started on the 'minus side of the line' and struggled to even secure a cleaning job in a foreign country. The 'minus side' presented me with huge odds: no family, church, friends, sponsor, inheritance or money in a bank account. Do I have anything going for me at all? What I had the world did not acknowledge, let alone respect or value. That is the world for you, different from God. Thank God, His yardstick for success is totally different! His ways are higher than man's.

Despite my initial disadvantages and setbacks, I have had the amazing privilege of travelling to Albania, Holland, Slovenia, America, Canada, Nigeria, India, United Emirates, Egypt, Tanzania, Hong Kong, South Africa, Uganda, Italy, Switzerland, Sweden, France, Spain, Greece and more. How? I dared to believe in God! With man this might be impossible, but with God all things are possible.

My incredible journey of faith started in my home country Kenya long before all of the above, when God raised me from the deathbed. Before the near-death experience, God had called me to England. Up until that time, it had not occurred to me to travel abroad, so I had no passport or cash stashed up somewhere.

My trauma due to the illness and the healing afterwards created a transformation in me and confirmed my calling! Like a resurrected Lazarus on a mission, I left Kenya with $100, no visa and a one-way ticket! When I eventually stepped on the other side of the immigration desk at Heathrow Airport, I had a year visa! It makes me cringe today when I look back but I was on God's mission and unafraid! Faith in the word of God had triumphed over the systems of man.

A pointer to my resolute faith in God is the fact that I have always allowed the word of God to challenge me even when I have doubt in my mind. One of my favourite scriptures is Romans 3: 4, 'Let God be true, but every man be a liar!' I may be defensive and self-justifying at first but I align myself with the word of God once the realisation dawns on me.

Annoyed and Defensive!

I remember the first day I heard someone in a non-church seminar quote 1 Timothy 6:10 (NIV), 'For the love of money is a root of all kinds of evil...'

My ears pricked up, especially when they said it didn't mean what I had always believed! That little voice in my head was now very loud, and it was asking all sorts of questions. My beliefs about money and God were being challenged, and I didn't like that one bit!

I didn't want to believe that he was right because I had heard that verse in all versions and paraphrases repeated countless times by people who couldn't even read! It had always meant the same thing, which this man was trying to say it didn't. I listened carefully with all my 'heresy' defences thinking, 'Why should I believe you? What do you know about the Bible? You're not even a preacher!' It's amazing how we can stand up for something we are not even sure of ourselves. When challenged, we assume the person challenging is wrong.

For me, two aspects of life have constantly 'reared their ugly heads' in a rather beautiful way when I least expect it: The areas of money (wealth) and my identity have always been a good 'thorn in the flesh' provoking my thinking. They tend to throw me off course a bit but strengthen my belief and resolve as I once regain absolute balance from pure perspective of God's word.

This book addresses the areas of money and wealth; it will challenge the status quo, the hand-me-down beliefs so many of us Christians carry around regarding money and wealth. These beliefs have an impact on the decisions we make, our outlook on life, attitudes, kingdom, and ministry and are crippling many faithful who are called by the Lord's name.

In this book I share principles I have tried, tested and proven to be true. It's not something I read in a book, it's my life and I have many witnesses to this glorious existence! Again, *let God be true and every man a liar.*

CHAPTER 1

I WILL BLESS YOU!

And you shall remember the LORD your God, for it is He who gives you power to get wealth, that He may establish His covenant which He swore to your fathers, as it is this day.

—Deuteronomy 8:18 (NKJV)

Who Cares?

Why is the relationship between money, God, and you important? Why should you care?

Put the above questions on pause for a moment and let's ruminate on perhaps a more important question, 'Was I born poor or not?' I don't believe anyone is born poor, no matter the family circumstances, location, race or creed! This assertion may sound like an irony coming from someone not born or raised in the developed world. I will do best here to justify my reasoning – with the word of God!

I was born in a little village on the slopes of Mount Kenya. When I was young, even having a pair of shoes signified wealth. While that is so far removed from the reality I live today and what I see now, the truth is, that little girl still lives in me; the values, beliefs, and doctrine that were instilled in me then, still reigns sometimes unchallenged!

I can remember one day while attending my Catholic primary school, I decided to wear my green canvas Bata shoes; it felt so good not to walk the three kilometres to school on sharp, hot rocks. Well, my history teacher didn't think so! He was offended and took it upon himself to remind me that flaunting wealth was not a good thing. I was punished for it, and after insults over my shoes and a stern reminder how low I truly was, he sent me outside to stand by the prominent tree where students from my class and other classes could see me! That's a double history lesson I will never forget, which may explain why I hated history so much in later years.

This was not just a lesson to me, but to everyone else in the class that flaunting wealth was bad, and those who display it should be attacked and punished. I was afraid to wear shoes to school and I guess every other child who witnessed my treatment. These types of wrong seeds were planted in some of us early in life. Then I and my school mates received such subtle loads of training to be poor. It wouldn't have mattered so much if we were born into a rich home in the same environment or in line for a wealth bequest. Our minds were conditioned for poverty.

My Pain and Struggles

My identity in Christ however opened the door to money and wealth for me, showing me the wealth in me and in nature around me. On the flip side as I grew in the Lord, it sometimes brought such contradiction and an inner struggle that was way too much to bear. I believe there were times when I pushed prosperity away because I was afraid it would drive me away from God! How wrong was I! If there were a comparison to what has the potential to drive me away from God more – wealth or poverty – I would say poverty is worse by a mile! Poverty has the power to make you question who God is as a provider. Most people struggling financially are so focused on what they don't have, that they don't have time to be grateful for what they have!

In 1996 I was in Albania on a long mission trip, I had left England on a faith high after witnessing a financial miracle. I had no money of my own; I didn't have friends, local church or a neighbour who I could call on to help finance my trip. I needed over £1,200, and I had to believe that God was Jehovah Jireh[i] and would provide for my every need. My fellow believers who were with me on the contrary thought I was asking for too much and told me they'd never seen it done before! I was being unreasonable and needed to look for other ways of funding the trip. Well, I didn't have anyone else but Him. I talked and prayed to God every day; I remember walking in the fields crying, shouting and expressing every kind of tantrum a little girl can have with her father.

In this struggle I had a revelation that changed my attitude towards God! It was then I realised I had been behaving, treating and expecting of God what I would of my earthly father. I was not acting out of absolute faith – a knowing that He was who He said He was! I believed it was my prayer, fasting and travailing that moved God. Things changed dramatically and I grew in my faith and my understanding of God the Father in that season. Needless to say, He provided more than I prayed for, including spending money for the duration of my trip.

On that trip to Albania, while minding my own business in the bathroom of my host family one day,

I heard an audible voice say, **'I have called you to a rich inheritance, I will bless you!'**

Shocked, I stood up and looked around; I was alone, so I asked out loud, 'Who's that?' In my spirit I knew who it was, I recognised that voice.

My relationship with God changed from that point; my faith for money against all odds experienced a deep impact, and while my journey and relationship with money had officially started in the spirit, my voice of reason (mind) was still on its own snail journey!

It took years for my mind to catch up with what had happened in the spirit in that season. I believe there is a process we have to go through to transition from *knowing* to *understanding* and finally *manifesting*. It took me years to awaken and realise that I was living in poverty in my mind without a conscious understanding.

It was the autumn of a particular year long after, and this particular Sunday morning I had gone to church, as is my usual custom. Unknown to me and probably other members in the congregation, the pastor had invited a man from a charity called Global Compassion. After the gentleman spoke, he said they were raising money to build winter shelters for Hungarian travellers so they wouldn't have to sleep out in the open during winter season. That sounded like a great project, which I wanted to give towards.

He asked those who could donate £100 to stand up, and at that moment, something very painful happened to me; I realised I didn't have £100 spare to give, so I couldn't stand up! Yes, I had a small child and all the many reasons I could give, but that was not it!

I was poor and living in justified poverty!

I could not give £100 to a needy person. I was upset with God, myself and the teachings of blessing that clearly were not working for me!

This was the moment my head caught up with the reality of 'rich inheritance' that I was not walking in. I had a harsh conversation with God and told him things had to change; this would be the last time this ever happened, and if my financial status didn't change, then I had no reason to believe the Bible.

As I write this I know without a shadow of a doubt: **God does not hold back wealth and prosperity from us**. He has released it to us, but we have been walking around repeating and teaching poverty doctrine (and how to believe it) to each other! Guard your heart above all else the scripture says; if you tell yourself the same lie over and over you will come to accept it as truth!

The words in the scripture below came after a painful period for the children of Israel; the people couldn't imagine how it would be possible to build a temple whose glory surpassed the previous one built by Solomon.

'...The silver is mine and the gold is mine, declares the Lord of Hosts' (**Haggai 2:8**).

The people were disappointed by the absence of precious metals needed to adorn the temple. Today there are many believers like the children of Israel living disappointed by the lack of the promised blessing, and feel they've believed in vain.

Many times we follow our senses blindly and create our reality on that basis but I believe we are missing the point. The power of God is beyond our senses and we can't comprehend that which we can't reason! For example, we pray for a miracle and when it happens, we say, 'I can't believe it!'

But know this, the Lord does not get caught up in our thinking and the mindset we develop because of a tragic event that took place in our lives.

He is faithful and will do what He said He would do no matter how unattainable it may seem to you. He did it with the temple and He will do same or similar for you and me in our lifetime!

Are you ready to believe Him to shake the universe?

CHAPTER 2

BIBLICAL PROSPERITY

Beloved, I pray that in every way you may prosper and enjoy good health, as your soul prospers.

—3 John 1:2

His Will

God's will for His people is that they prosper. This is clear in both the Old and the New Testament. I fail to understand at what point spirituality and wealth parted company, and we learnt to explain away the lack of prosperity as a standard expectation for believers. The phrase 'too spiritual for any earthly good' comes to mind and seems to be at work here.

Many people have separated spirituality from prosperity and do a very good job of keeping it that way. Even when they read it in the Bible, they say it's talking about spiritual prosperity. What is so sad about this approach is that those same people seem to struggle with poverty and cannot understand why God does not bless them.

The contradiction and conflict going through the mind over this matter are only explained with more self-deception. No one will contradict themselves; and whatever his or her core belief or value is, it will always triumph subconsciously.

What is referred to as self-sabotage in psychology is nothing more than core beliefs operating in the subconscious to stop you from contradicting your underlying personal beliefs!

Let's explore some scriptures:

'But the word is very near you, in your mouth and in your heart, that you may observe it. See, **I have set before you today life and prosperity,** *and death and adversity'* **(Deuteronomy 30:14-15).**

This scripture is compounded in that it not only sets God's heart for us His people, but also tells us how it really works!

The word is very near you and in your heart, what are you meant to do with this word? In the slogan of a famous brand, just do it! There is no hidden mystery or doctrine to be observed.

The words out of your mouth are the currency that you live by!

How often have you thought about the words you speak, analysed each one of them before speaking them? There are many references in the Bible concerning the power of spoken words but for now, let us focus on the scripture above. The words are in your mouth and heart; choose *life and prosperity* or *death and adversity*! The choice is in the words out of your mouth and heart not something out there driven by someone else.

'*A good man out of the good treasure of his heart* **brings forth** *that* **which is good**; *and an evil man out of the evil treasure of his heart* **brings forth that which is evil**: *for out of the abundance of the heart his mouth speaks*' *(Luke 6:45).*

If you knew that every word that comes out of your mouth creates either prosperity or adversity, would you be more careful?

One thing I love about the Bible is that it uses repetition to assert a point; the words in

Deuteronomy are repeated in the book of Luke in the New Testament. If these words are not important, they would not be repeated in the New Testament. There are people who consider the Old Testament (OT) as old and not relevant which is sad. Jesus referred to the OT as 'the commandment of God' (Matthew 15:3) and as the 'Word of God' (Mark 7:13). He also indicated that it was indestructible: 'Until Heaven and earth pass away, not the smallest letter or stroke shall pass away from the law, until all is accomplished' (Matthew 5:18).

Is Prosperity From God?

Prosperity is in God's heart where His people are concerned. Prosperity is mentioned numerous times in the Old Testament, and in the New Testament Jesus also reminded His followers of this truth. If that wasn't enough, Apostle Paul brought it up again when he said:

'I pray that in every way you may prosper and enjoy good health, as your soul prospers.'

Prosperity is God's universal design and it has no boundaries!

I was having a conversation with a friend about money and being prosperous, and she went on to quote the scripture about money being the root of all evil. I could not help but point out that statistically, in areas where people have less money, there is higher crime rate, poor health, illiteracy, premature death, to name a few of the social issues in such places.

People that live in those areas, for example, in London where I am based, tend to pay higher insurance premiums for every service because there is a higher crime rate and an expectation that insurance companies may end up paying out against the policy.

On the other hand, in the more affluent areas where residents have more wealth, the insurance premiums are low, and queues at hospitals are shorter because they can afford private medical healthcare.

What does this show us where money is concerned? Does it really bring evil or good?

If poverty or lack of money is such a good and godly thing, why does it have such a negative impact on the community? Is this God's will for us?

Here's that scripture that has taken many a potential millionaire to the grave penniless!

'For the **love of money is the root of all evil**: which some coveted after, they have erred from the faith, and pierced themselves through with many sorrows' (*I Timothy 6:10*).

Now look at the scripture based on what you read above, and see if you can identify where the problem is. The majority of us, if not all of us, think more about money when we don't have it and will do anything to get it.

So the issue that leads to evil is not having money but the lack of it! I've had issues where people never repaid the money I lent them, giving long stories why they can't pay - and it's always people who don't have enough!

Strangely, they don't learn; they still come back wanting more with long stories!

Poor people like to speak out against those that have money and say all sorts of unkind things; however statistically, there are more poor people in prison for money-related crimes than there are wealthy people.

I am here to tell you that God's will for you is to be prosperous! Remember, it's a choice you have to make. Choose the words you speak and the meditations of your heart carefully, according to the book of Deuteronomy, selecting prosperity principles that apply to your life.

The lies that 'money is the root of evil by having it' has been going on for so long, but I want you to open your eyes and ears to hear what the Spirit of God is saying to you through the words of this book.

God's will is for you to prosper, have good health, enjoy abundance, family union and a sense of community.

King David, a character from the Bible, was a man that walked in prosperity to the highest level, and he wrote about it. He remained a humble man where his relationship with God was concerned, and never forgot his humble beginnings.

David wrote below:

*'Let the LORD be magnified, **who has pleasure in the prosperity of his servant'** (Psalm 35:27).*

The Lord has pleasure, and even takes delight in your prosperity! Imagine a delighted God watching you prosper!

At times, we all get lost in our thoughts and ideologies that we've bought from other people and wonder where God is, and David was no different. He had to remind his own soul that the Lord had given him abundance!

'Return unto your rest, O my soul; for the LORD **has dealt bountifully with you**' (Psalm 116:7).

The children of Israel were coming back home after exile and God had something on His mind; He made the following promise to His people on their return to a land that looked desolate and so very different from what they remembered.

"*Again, proclaim, saying, 'Thus says the LORD of hosts,* **My cities will again overflow with prosperity**...'" *(Zechariah 1:17).*

Wherever you find yourself today, God wants to make the same promise that no matter how bad things look in your life; He wants to see you overflow with prosperity!

'It is the blessing of the LORD that makes rich, and He adds no sorrow to it' (**Proverbs 10:22**).

'Furthermore, as for every man to whom **God has given riches and wealth,** *He has also empowered him to eat from them and to receive his*

reward and rejoice in his labour; this is the gift of God' **(Ecclesiastes 5:19).**

Deuteronomy 28: 1-6 (NLT):

'If you fully obey the LORD your God and carefully keep all his commands that I am giving you today, the LORD your God will set you high above all the nations of the world.

You will experience all these blessings if you obey the LORD your God:

Your towns and your fields will be blessed.

Your children and your crops will be blessed.

The offspring of your herds and flocks will be blessed.

Your fruit baskets and breadboards will be blessed.

Wherever you go and whatever you do, you will be blessed.'

Poverty is a curse!

Many years ago, I didn't know the power of the words written in the Bible so God, in His infinite wisdom, brought a certain book my way! That book and one other are what set me on a foundation of my rights as a believer! The words I read shook me and burned into my soul, for as strange as they sounded my spirit was bearing witness with them. I felt hope rising; I was like the Eunuch in the book of Acts who had been reading the Bible without understanding! Kenneth Hagin, the author whom I did not know, became like Philip to me – my first virtual spiritual mentor teaching me the rights to a long-ago covenant that gave me rights!

Using scriptures, Kenneth Hagin took me through the Old and New Testament showing me step by step why poverty was a curse. I didn't dare tell anyone, for we believers seem to think poverty is godly! 'What you don't have here in this realm you shall get in heaven, hallelujah!' – That is heresy and not of God!

This little book, titled *Redeemed from Poverty, Sickness, and Spiritual Death by Kenneth E. Hagin*[i], written many years ago deals and explains scriptures on the three subjects: poverty, sickness and spiritual death. It gives examples and testimonies where they had been applied in the Bible. It was through this book that my faith in these areas took root. I began to understand two correlated relationships—one with Jehovah-Rapha[ii] and the other with disease and what to do to sever the latter and solidify the former.

Like most things, you improve with practice – and spiritual laws are the same. It requires faith to believe in the first place, and continuing the practice requires discipline. These two qualities are not natural and require a working at, and most people give up way too easily. If they believe in something and they don't see results, they conclude it doesn't work – how wrong is that attitude!

It was no different for me as a young believer; I suffered many fears over pleasing God, shame, guilt of sin, and living righteously. I knew in my head I was right with God, but I didn't understand it in my spirit, and wondered if truly I had been set free from the law of poverty because poverty was all around me! Could it be that easy?

While your overall faith in God may not be relevant to the topic of this book, it is fundamental to know your rights as a believer, because if you do not have the foundations in your faith, you are going to struggle. Imagine if the greatest architect builds a house without foundation; it doesn't matter how magnificent it looks on the outside, its life is short and there is great danger to the occupants. That house is unstable and can collapse any moment. That's how it works; put simply, your foundation in the word of God is paramount to what else you build in your walk with Him.

Now back to the subject of poverty!

Reading Kenneth Hagin's book was a real challenge to me, as much as I wanted to believe. Living in Africa, I had not only witnessed extreme poverty around me, but was no stranger to it and up until that point I didn't know I had power over it!

According to **Deuteronomy 28** there are many blessings to be had, but with it goes the curse of poverty upon God's children if they disobeyed Him. Contrary to what has been taught for many years in religious doctrine, it is very clear in the Old Testament that poverty and lack were never viewed as a blessing from God! Poverty or lack of blessing, were deemed as a curse.

What is your core belief on this? What thoughts come to mind when you think about having a lot of money? Do you feel condemned in any way? Can you track back to when you started believing this?

These questions are great in helping you identify and uproot any un-supporting beliefs concerning money and wealth!

I would like to skip the words in Deuteronomy 28:15-18, 38-40 and the likes which are not always ecouraging; however, this is the mistake we sometimes make. We only take the good and leave what is uncomfortable and when it happens we don't recognise it! There are always two sides to the coin, which brings me to this other natural law – the Law of Duality. You will find it in operation in the story of creation, and again all through the scriptures there are examples of the Law of Duality at work. When you think about it, even in your everyday life, if for any reason you don't undertake a task that is meant to bring you a natural benefit, you will receive the opposite.

If you are excited and ready to receive the blessing in Deuteronomy 28: 1-12, then you might as well know what the other side offers. It's important that when given options on anything, you know exactly what is included in each option, so you are making an informed decision. God doesn't spring things up on us – He tells us clearly like a good father the consequences of our decision.

Deuteronomy 28: 15 – 20 (NLT):

'But if you refuse to listen to the LORD your God and do not obey all the commands and decrees I

am giving you today, all these curses will come and overwhelm you:
Your towns and your fields will be cursed.
Your fruit baskets and breadboards will be cursed.
Your children and your crops will be cursed.
The offspring of your herds and flocks will be cursed.
Wherever you go and whatever you do, you will be cursed.
The LORD himself will send on you curses, confusion, and frustration in everything you do until at last you are completely destroyed for doing evil and abandoning me.'

There are people who have taken these scriptures and used them to question God's love and while God is too big for me to defend, it is important to realise there are universal laws in operation in this universe we call home, and they are no respecter of any person. When you understand these laws and make them work for you, it will help you walk in freedom!

It took me a long time to figure this universal law thing out and how it worked, but it has set me free!

'Today I have given you the choice between life and death, between blessings and curses. Now I call on heaven and earth to witness the choice you make.

Oh, that you would choose life so that you and your descendants might live' (**Deuteronomy 30: 19** NLT)

We've been redeemed from the Curse

I am glad to see you are still reading after the heavy stuff in the previous section! Remember this, God always provides a way out; that's how deep His love for us is!

As a new covenant believer, I used to struggle with all the laws in the Old Testament; my desire to read the Bible from cover to cover ended when I got to all the laws, and I gave up. This was for several reasons: I didn't understand the culture, did not identify with them, and I found it impossible to ever fulfil them.

I felt doomed most times as redemption was through sacrifice; however, Apostle Paul's letter to the Galatians cleared that up for me – Christ had redeemed me from the curse of the law! And this is for you too!

'But Christ has rescued us from the curse pronounced by the law. When he was hung on the cross, he took upon himself the curse for our wrongdoing. For it is written in the Scriptures,

'cursed is everyone who is hung on a tree.' (Galatians 3:13 NLT)

Stop the Money and Mammon Talk!

In all my English-speaking years, I have never heard the word 'mammon' used anywhere in any context outside of church circles! I could be the only one with this experience, however, since I live within the realm of the English language, there's a big chance I am not the only one.

But what exactly does 'mammon' mean? The word MAMMON and MONEY are used interchangeably in different translations of the Bible — in which case one could say they mean the same thing. The word is found in Matthew 6:24. However, what we hear repeated most is the part about serving two masters. In doing research on this word 'mammon,' I found it interesting that it does not have a direct source, and therefore it is unclear what it meant originally, yet we whip it around like candy and have created a doctrine out of it!

We suffer from a condition I call *single verse syndrome* that tells what we want to say and hear, but only telling a part of the truth. Many have suffered disappointment, frustration and have abandoned the faith believing it doesn't work, and this takes me to a rebuke God sent to the priests through the Prophets Hosea, Isaiah, Jeremiah, and others:

'My people are destroyed for lack of knowledge. Because you have rejected knowledge, I also will reject you from being my priest' **(Hosea 4:6a NASB).**

Let's see what *Isaiah says,*

Therefore My people go into exile for their lack of knowledge; And their honorable men are famished, And their multitude is parched with thirst **(Isaiah 5:13 NASB).**

and Jeremiah,

Then I said, "They are only the poor, They are foolish; For they do not know the way of the LORD Or the ordinance of their God. **(Jeremiah 5:4 NASB).**

Today, in the world, we have access to the scriptures in many forms, and, therefore, it is not your minister, pastor, priest, vicar or guru's responsibility to hand down the knowledge you need as it were back in the day of the prophets mentioned above!

Matthew 6:24 is part of a much longer teaching Jesus delivered now known as 'The Sermon on the Mount.' It covers a lot of issues, and Jesus used his usual repetitive style to signify the importance of the message, by teaching the same principle using different examples to drive the point home:

*'The **lamp of the body is the eye**. If therefore your eye is good, your whole body will be full of light. But if your eye is bad, your whole body will be full of darkness. If therefore the light that is in you is darkness, how great is that darkness!*
***No one can serve two masters**; for either he will hate the one and love the other, or else he will be loyal to the one and despise the other.* **You cannot serve God and mammon.**
***Therefore I say to you, do not worry about your life**, what you will eat or what you will drink; nor about your body, what you will put on. Is not life more than food and the body more than clothing?'*
(Matthew 6: 22-25 KJV)

The majority of the Bible translations use the word 'money' instead of 'mammon,' and others use 'riches'. The immediate verse after the use of the word 'mammon' starts with 'therefore' to mean there is a connection between the two verses. Interestingly, the continuation is about not worrying about life! A reassurance about God's provision and order of things. Jesus did not dwell on verse 24 'mammon/money' but continued to teach about trusting God, emphasising this principle, concluding with verse 33:

'But seek first the kingdom of God and His righteousness, and all these things shall be added to you' (KJV).

My question to you is this: 'Why does this one verse have to be used as the ticket to poverty if Jesus didn't focus on it?' Jesus focused more on a godly 'done for you' type of provision from God, as is the case with the 'birds of the air.' He didn't dwell on the 'not having or having too much', but instead, he dealt with the mindset that constantly worries about lack and poverty.

These verses in Matthew 6 are shedding light on God's heart where you and I are concerned, where our priority, focus, and trust should lie. Yes, the inability to serve two masters is a principle that applies across the board; wealth and riches happen to be the ones mentioned here.

In Kenya we have a proverb that says *'if you cook two pots of food at the same time, you will burn one'.*

I have proved this to myself many times in the kitchen and in daily tasks: If you attempt multiple tasks at the same time, you will notice that while it may feel good, something will get compromised – either left incomplete, or ruined!

While theologians debate and argue about the structure of the Sermon on the Mount, you and I need to focus on the application of it – why was Jesus teaching it, and what did He want his listeners to learn? What was the relevance of it, and how does it apply to your life today?

I stand by this claim: GOD NEVER CONTRADICTS HIMSELF! He doesn't say one thing through one prophet and then change it through the next one. He will not say He will bless you and then tell you the same blessing is evil! It is always important to test every word coming to you, and contradiction is one way of knowing whether to take it seriously or not.

Money, possessions, and riches are external and as it is often said, 'Whatever you focus on grows' and becomes your object of desire, ruling you! Wealth in itself is not innately evil; it all depends on whose hand it is in.

Riches, wealth, and possessions magnify who YOU are in character as a person; on their own they do not have the power to induce alien behaviour or turn you into something you are not.

Let me illustrate the point I'm making using one of the basic human needs – shelter. The majority of people have shelter, though it might vary from 'cardboard box' to a luxury mansion and beyond. While these are two ends of the spectrum, they are meeting the same need. If a 'house' in itself were evil, then that would make all houses evil, regardless of what end of the spectrum they are on.

That's a concept most people would have an adverse reaction to, based on our pre-conceived ideas about this subject; however, if we remove the bias in a discussion or argument as it may be perceived, we can weigh up things objectively.

While there may be a case for everything in moderation, remember the definition of moderation differs from person to person, and that's what makes all the difference in the outcome.
If we apply the same argument to money or wealth, it is not the amount of money that determines how we behave; it is who we are, our values, beliefs, and priorities that determine how others see us.

If they see **self-indulgence**, then it's a character that you already possess that is being brought to light. What I have observed is this: we humans are consistent. We are consistent and will portray the same behaviour in every aspect of our lives may it be at a smaller degree depending on the circumstances.

We can safely conclude that God does not have a problem with His people being wealthy and prosperous; as a matter of fact, it is His desire.

He is a God of abundance; just look at nature and see how plants produce! I don't know of any one plant that produces a single fruit per season; they over-produce the bloom ensuring that even when some drop off, there is still enough for a good harvest!

'And if God cares so wonderfully for wildflowers that are here today and thrown into the fire tomorrow, He will certainly care for you. Why do you have so little faith?

Seek the Kingdom of God above all else, and live righteously, and He will give you everything you need' **(Matthew 6:30,33 NLT).**

What is God's will?

'Beloved, I pray that in every way you may prosper and enjoy good health, as your soul prospers' **(3 John 1:2).**

CHAPTER 3

BIBLICAL HALL OF WEALTH

*Furthermore, as for every man to whom **God has given riches and wealth**, He has also empowered him to eat from them and to receive his reward and rejoice in his labour; this is the gift of God.* — Ecclesiastes 5:19

Flaunt It!

The Bible is full of God-loving men and women flaunting wealth, though not in the same way we see today. What I find interesting is that we don't seem to want to discuss their material wealth – it's like a taboo that goes against spirituality. If I mention that a certain man like Abraham was very rich, I am met with the word 'but' which to me, says that person refuses to focus on 'the fleeting things of this world' where their faith and values are concerned. The spirituality of the patriarchs seems to be the only subject of discussion within Christendom!

Over the years I have come to recognise that there is a correlation between wealth and relationship with God. If you go through the books of (I & II) Kings, you will notice that those kings who served the Lord were materially blessed and it is expressly stated. Prior to the kings of Israel, we have the patriarchs who were also very rich and prosperous.

It is important for us to understand this and live according to it. The scriptures tell us that God doesn't have favourites, contrary to what some believe. Do you think the scripture below refers to you?

> *'I now truly understand that God does not show favouritism, but welcomes those from every nation who fear Him and do what is right'* (Acts: 10:34 BSB).

This same message is repeated in the book of Romans – no matter how we look at it, it is clear you are in line for God's abundant blessings just like Abraham, David, and many others were! What He did for them, He will do for you and me, but we must first believe in order to receive!

'For God does not show favouritism' **(Romans 2:11 NLT).**

Christ Jesus said: 'A thief comes only to steal and to kill and to destroy. I have come so that they may have life and have it in abundance' **(John 10:10 HCSB).**

Do not entertain the thought of a less abundant life or allow yourself to be robbed of the blessing that is rightfully yours!

Job

The name Job for Bible readers only brings one topic to mind – suffering! But is that what the book is really about? It is true there is too much suffering for anyone's liking, but the book does raise some pertinent questions regarding the topic of suffering which is evergreen, generation to generation.

Let's leave the 'suffering' part of Job's story and move on to our focus subject: Money, GOD and You. What does the story of Job teach us concerning wealth and God?

I wish to point out that the pronoun 'you' is used to speak to *you*, and to bring these principles and facts relevant to you. There are many times I've read books, listened to sermons and thought of the person who would benefit from it. How wrong this approach is! The minute you think it's good for someone else, you will not benefit from it because your mind closes the door.

When I read the story of Job, two things captivate me: his spirituality and wealth! The story starts with setting the scene of who this man is so we don't jump to judgmental conclusion. It sounds to me like this, 'Before you come to any conclusion, let me tell you the kind of man we are talking about here.' This only becomes obvious in the latter part of the book during Job's interaction with his friends about his personal character. In all honesty, most of us would be exactly the same as his friends!

'There was a man in the land of Uz, whose name was Job; and that man was **blameless and upright,** *and* **one who feared God** *and shunned evil'* **(Job 1: 1 NKJV).**

Now that we know about his spirituality, let's look at what he owned – in today's terms, it would be 'let's look at your house, your car and all things that speak of prosperity.' Can we handle that?

'He had seven sons and three daughters, and he owned seven thousand sheep, three thousand camels, five hundred yoke of oxen and five hundred donkeys, and had a large number of servants. He was the greatest man among all the people of the East' **(Job 1: 2-3 NIV).**

Cleary this man, Job, was wealthy – we are talking millions in today's terms! You have to have land to accommodate all that flock, and it has to be large enough to provide pasture. Oh, I forgot to mention the workforce to look after it and their shelter too; and in those days, workers moved in with the boss!

This is the man who has the cheek to say he's right and he knows he hasn't done anything wrong. If you were one of Job's friends, what kind of things would be coming to your mind concerning his sickness?

I was once very ill on the deathbed, and you would be amazed how quickly people come to a conclusion why you are sick and what you should do.

Job's wealth was not limited to him alone; his children were blessed too. They would throw parties at their homes and make merry. Talking about wealth that extends to generations!

In Job's story, everything starts to change in his life when Satan appears on the scene and starts to accuse God over Job. Note this: it wasn't God saying, 'Job and his children are having too much fun; let me teach them a lesson.' The first attack was to his wealth, and it came from outside, not from God. The scripture says that devil is the accuser of the brethren, an art he's perfected very well and we should be aware of this!

Why wealth before health?

'Have you not put a hedge around him and his household and everything he has? You have blessed the work of his hands, so that his flocks and herds are spread throughout the land' **(Job 1: 10 NIV)**.

When we feel under attack, and things are going wrong, we need to bear in mind that Satan is still at work. (I didn't write this for you to start obsessing with the devil though.) The book of Revelation calls him *the accuser of the brethren,* something he loves to do – to challenge our relationship with God. God has no need of punishing you; He created you and loves you unconditionally!

Job lost everything, including his children, but he never lost his relationship with God. It is important that we understand what holds true – the order of things in our lives.

After what seems like endless suffering and discussions, God shows up! And guess what He does? He set the record right by putting everyone in their place, and goes on to restore everything Job had!

It wasn't easy for Job to stand his ground while everyone close to him was telling him things contrary to what his heart felt.

I don't know what you've been through or are going through, but I have this one question: 'Have you lost material things or have you lost your faith in God?'

There are times when, like Job, you wonder where God is, based on what is going on in your life.

If only I knew where to find God, I would go to his court. (**Job 23:3 NLT**).

I find we are too afraid to tell God exactly what we think and feel because we don't want to offend Him. I learnt this simple truth many years ago; I might as well tell Him what's running through my mind and heart because He knows it anyway! It feels so much better airing it out!

Finally, in Job 38, God shows up (and it's at this point I would want to crawl under a rock and hide if I were Job), for God puts everything said and done into perspective.

Where do wealth and prosperity come from? Contrary to what many believers think, Job 42 brings us nicely to the source of wealth with absolute clarity. God is not against wealth; He gives it.

'After Job had prayed for his friends, **the Lord restored his fortunes and gave him twice as much** *as he had before'* (Job 42:10 NIV).

'The Lord blessed the latter part of Job's life more than the former part. *He had fourteen thousand sheep, six thousand camels, a thousand yoke of oxen and a thousand donkeys. And he also had seven sons and three daughters'* (Job 42:12-13 NIV).

Abraham

This man, Abraham, is one of my favourite Bible characters – I suppose because I identify with him perhaps more than anyone else. But who is Abraham, and why do several world religions fight over him?

Abraham's birth name is Abram, son of Terah. He was born in the land of Ur, but most of his experiences in the Bible are of a nomad God-believing man who we see wandering from place to place living in tents. According to Genesis, Abram was in Haran when he got the call from God at age 75, to leave his home and family behind and follow God into a strange land that God would give him!

*"The Lord had said to Abram, '**Go from your country, your people and your father's household** to the land I will show you.*
'I will make you into a great nation, and I will bless you;
I will make your name great, and you will be a blessing.
I will bless those who bless you, and whoever curses you I will curse;
and all peoples on earth will be blessed through you'" **(Genesis 12: 1-3 NIV).**

This is what makes me start paying attention to this crazed man, for it says a lot about him; he chose to leave his family to follow *'a voice in his head'.*

I come from an African ancestral community, and I can imagine his family, elders and the community at large trying to persuade him not to go with words like; *'You are a little too old to be running away from home!'* He would have to deal with the fear of curses, losing an inheritance, the expectations, rituals and ceremonies that would go to a son and later grandchildren.

He was a married man – what did his wife Sarah think? Some of the details are left to our imagination, but as a woman, I can imagine the uncomfortable conversations between husband and wife, with both her family and husband wanting her to take their sides. Later in the story though, we do see Sarah's character of obedience to her husband.

Abram embarked on a faith journey to the unknown. He took his wife, Lot, his nephew, and his possessions and departed. We are not told of a farewell party, but he was determined to follow God's call.

Abram headed south into the land of Canaan, a land inhabited by a warrior people called the Canaanites. He settled temporarily in Shechem and Bethel, and it was here that God told Abraham his descendants would inherit the Canaanite land.

Abraham was a fascinating man; Apostle Paul said this of him:

> *'For he was looking forward to the city with foundations, whose architect and builder is God'* **(Hebrews 11:10).**

Like Job, we see the blessing of God over Abraham's life! From when God called him, He made a promise to bless him, and to increase him in every area of his life. At the time, this looked far-fetched; he and his wife had no children, and they both were going to be living a nomadic life.

Yet true to His word, God made good His promise!

> *'Now Abram was very rich in livestock, in silver and in gold'* **(Genesis 13:2 NASB).**

Many years after Abraham's crazy faith move, he sent his servant to get a wife for his son Isaac, and this is the servant's report concerning Abraham:

'And the LORD has greatly blessed my master; he has become a wealthy man. The LORD has given him flocks of sheep and goats, herds of cattle, a fortune in silver and gold, and many male and female servants and camels and donkeys' **(Genesis 24:35).**

There is no explaining away Abraham's wealth, and now we know that through our faith in Christ Jesus we have become heirs of Abraham's covenant. We receive that same promise, an inheritance of a man who was extremely rich, successful and prosperous in everything he had!

'He redeemed us in order that the blessing given to Abraham might come to the Gentiles through Christ Jesus, so that by faith we might receive the promise of the Spirit' **(Galatians 3:14 NIV).**

There are many wealthy biblical figures such that I would not be able to include them all in this book, but I am going to add a short note here concerning Isaac, the son of Abraham, who equally was blessed in his own right. Wealth is generational, and we are to teach our children how to acquire wealth, not just hand it down with no wisdom.

'Now Isaac sowed in that land and reaped in the same year a hundredfold. And the LORD blessed him, and the man became rich, and continued to grow richer until he became very wealthy; for he had possessions of flocks and herds and a great household, so that the Philistines envied him' **(Genesis 26:12 – 14m NASB).**

David

We read about David in the New Testament and marvel at this man who had a unique relationship with God. Yet he started as a shepherd, a child who was despised and regarded an outcast by his own family. We first encounter the young boy David out in the field; his father doesn't even call him home when the prophet visits.

*"After removing Saul, he made David their king. God testified concerning him: 'I have found **David son of Jesse, a man after my own heart; he will do everything I want him to do***'"* (Acts 13:22 NIV).

Unlike Job who fought for his self-righteousness, David knew his human frailty and his unending errors. There are so many examples of his failures and you must wonder whether he's the same one God referred to as a man after His own heart!

One thing David did very well was repentance; he would put his hand up and admit when he was wrong and expect punishment. When you look at Psalm 51 you see his brokenness, a realisation that he's messed up and deserved punishment. He knew that merciful character of God and always chose to be under the hand of God.

David would do what God wanted him to do, but he also loved to worship God. Today, we read the many songs and poetry he wrote from the heart. When he brought the Ark of the Covenant back to Jerusalem, he danced before the Lord until his robe fell off! His wife was mad at him for his behaviour but this didn't bother David.

Oh, I wish we had this freedom to worship God in spirit and in truth without a care about other people! These are some of the attributes that separated David from all others. God loved him so much that He promised that there would always be a king in the house of Judah from his lineage.

'The LORD watches over the blameless all their days, and their inheritance will last forever' **(Psalm 37:18 HCSB).**

There are many times we think we are not good enough, giving reasons why we can't be blessed. David is a good example that God is not a respecter of persons. If you compare him to his predecessor, King Saul, there are many differences in background, skills, stature and attitude of the heart.

Saul didn't care much about what God said, and in the end, this cost him his family and kingdom.
David's life is full of abundance, so there would be way too many scriptures to include; however, one of the things he desired to do was build a temple for God. God told him since he was a man of war and

had shed much blood; his son was going to build the temple. David's heart desired to build this temple, so he did the next best thing – he started collecting building materials for his son! This is what he said about that one offering to the Lord:

'I have worked hard to provide materials for building the Temple of the LORD - nearly 4,000 tons of gold, 40,000 tons of silver, and so much iron and bronze that it cannot be weighed. I have also gathered timber and stone for the walls, though you may need to add more' **(1 Chronicles 22:14 NLT).**

In my opinion, with all the noise I hear today about preachers accumulating wealth, none of them can touch David on that one, so it's about time the naysayers started accumulating their own! This was a man after God's own heart! Purpose and motivation for the accumulation are key, however, only God knows the motives of the heart so let's leave the judging to Him.

At the end of his life, David the shepherd boy made a statement below that we should all take to heart and truly know who our Provider is:

'I was young and now I am old, yet I have never seen the righteous forsaken or their children begging bread' **(Psalm 37:25 (NIV).**

We are God's righteous, and He promises that He will never leave us or forsake us! He is our refuge and strong tower at all times!

'And he [David] died in a good old age, full of days, riches, and honour: and Solomon his son reigned in his stead' **(1 Chronicles 29:28).**

King Solomon

A note on King Solomon, David's son and his successor: Here we see another example where wealth is being passed down, and the heir making it in his own right.
Sadly, we do sometimes sneer at those that have inherited wealth and fail to see that the majority of them would have been taught the prosperity principles.

'So King Solomon became richer and wiser than any other king on earth. Kings from every nation came to consult him and to hear the wisdom God had given him' **(2 Chronicles 9:22 – 23 NLT)**.

As I write this about Solomon, the verse below comes to mind, one that you need to meditate on, as you can't have that which you curse even in your thoughts! The English say *'walls have ears!'*

'Curse not the king, no not in thy thought; and curse not the rich in thy bedchamber: for a bird of the air shall carry the voice, and that which hath wings shall tell the matter' **(Ecclesiastes 10:20 KJV)**.

Jacob

The men and women of the Bible fascinate me; they are like characters in a movie sometimes running out to go and change before the next scene. They come in all shapes and sizes and represent all of us at any given time. The Bible is very personal to me; I play each role at different seasons of my life, and depending on what's going on, I will resonate with one character over the other.

Jacob was the younger twin to Esau, Abraham's grandchildren. They had an interesting co-existence; they started fighting before they were born – worrying the mother! We will not go in-depth on that, but do read their full story in the book of Genesis.

> *'But when the infants kept on wrestling each other inside her womb, she asked herself, 'Why is this happening?' So she asked the LORD for an explanation'* **(Genesis 25: 22 ISV).**

The twins are very different in their life choices and their strange kind of sibling banter, as you would expect. A very strange event happens in their life when Esau hands over his birthright to Jacob for a bowl of soup because he was very hungry!

The 'so what' generation might be saying 'what's the big deal?' but it truly *is* a big deal! The big lesson here: be careful about those spur-of-a-moment decisions we sometimes make without realising the full price! That decision cost Esau his inheritance and Jacob had to run for his life, and we pick up his story of wealth from there. *(Read the full details in Genesis 25: 27 - 34).*

Jacob, on his lonesome journey to his uncle and fearing for his life, had a spiritual encounter that changed his life, and that of generations to come:

"As he slept, he dreamed of a stairway that reached from the earth up to heaven. And he saw the angels of God going up and down the stairway. At the top of the stairway stood the LORD, and he said, 'I am the LORD, the God of your grandfather Abraham, and the God of your father, Isaac. The ground you are lying on belongs to you. I am giving it to you and your descendants'" **(Genesis 28: 12 – 13 NLT).**

So after this experience, Jacob continued on the journey and got to his uncle Laban who later learnt to be quite cunning; a real match to Jacob's deceitful character. He fell in love with his cousin Rachel and wanted to marry her. After working 7 years to pay dowry, Laban tricked Jacob and gave him Leah the elder sister on the wedding night! Jacob had to work another 7 years for Rachel's dowry. You trick someone, you get tricked back (the law of sowing and reaping at work). What a drama!

In all this time we see Jacob working for Laban, he was not relying on inheritance; he had to build his own wealth as he had to leave everything with Esau. He only managed to run away with his life, birth right but no possessions and had to start all over again!

This phenomenon of having to start all over is more common than you would think! So if you find that you've lost everything and you have to start again, don't despair. Success can be learnt and is also transferrable, go back and look at what you did to achieve success the previous time.

Jacob worked many years and continued to trust God; he listened to the unorthodox advice that came to him through dreams and the result was abundance.

'As a result, Jacob became very wealthy, with large flocks of sheep and goats, female and male servants, and many camels and donkeys' **(Genesis 30:43 NLT).**

Despite the birth right disaster where Jacob seemed to have every blessing 'deceitfully' handed to him, both brothers were abundantly blessed with livestock and possession. In the Old Testament livestock was the currency signifying abundance, as you will have seen in the earlier sections of this chapter.

'Esau took his wives, his children, and his entire household, along with his livestock and cattle—all the wealth he had acquired in the land of Canaan—and moved away from his brother, Jacob. There was not enough land to support them both because of all the livestock and possessions they had acquired' **(Genesis 36:6-7 NLT).**

CHAPTER 4

PROSPERITY PRINCIPLES

> *I call heaven and earth as witnesses today against you, that I have set before you life and death, blessing and cursing. Therefore choose life, that both you and your descendants may live.*
> —**Deuteronomy 30:19**

It's A Deal!

What do you say when God lays a covenant like this before you and all you have to do is choose? Most of us would say, 'Just choose – what's the big deal!' But when you look at the backdrop to this covenant, you will understand why it may not have been as easy as you might think.

Very few of us living today have any experience of what it feels like to be a slave, and so when we read the account of the children of Israel leaving Egypt, it's just a nice story that is not relevant. But if you look past that, you will see the condition of the human heart being addressed; the things that mattered to them still matter to us today. Their struggles are our struggles in another guise, but the heart responds in exactly the same way.

They had been slaves for generations; their history maybe a little distorted from hand-me-down stories, so blaming the ancestors may have been at play here. Finally, the big moment comes, and they are leaving, but they have no earthly possessions! No silver, no gold and definitely no diamonds!

The fact is this: money in your pocket gives you confidence! You know if anything goes wrong you can take care of it. As my grandmother used to say, 'You must make sure you take money with you just in case you break someone's egg' (at the market)!

God knows our inner desires and the need for confidence, He devised a plan to make sure the tired, weary slaves were not walking away empty handed. They needed a confidence boost and a sign that God was with them for they had been down for so long. Even the mere fact that the Egyptians gave them their gold and silver willingly would have been enough of a sign from God that He wanted more for them beyond how they perceived themselves.

'Now the sons of Israel had done according to the word of Moses, for they had requested from the Egyptians **articles of silver and articles of gold***, and clothing; and the LORD had given the people favour in the sight of the Egyptians, so that* **they let them have their request***'* (Exodus 12:35-36 NASB).

King David picked up on the importance of this principle in the Psalm below:

'And he brought them forth with silver and gold, and there was not one sick person among their tribes' (Psalm 105:37).

Most of the time, where prosperity is concerned, we are coming from a place of lack that we don't know what the real truth is for ourselves. If you have wondered whether it is possible for you to prosper, I am here to tell you that the same God who worked on behalf of the children of Israel and proved Himself faithful wants you to win in your life as well.

You may look back at your family line and say, 'No one in my family has ever been wealthy for generations,' and even when you look at your community, you are struggling to find wealth there either. And you may ask, 'How is it possible?'

Look at the situation the children of Israel were in – slaves, treated poorly, looked down upon, outcasts, put down – and so it was hard to accept prosperity principles, yet God had to start them somewhere.

Your journey starts with accepting that God wants you to prosper. It is a change of mindset that is absolutely necessary, a paradigm shift!

The prosperity principles in this book were not set in place by your family, community, country or anyone else that come to your mind. They belong to God who put them in place; only he is in absolute control and says they rightfully belong to you! I dare you to challenge yourself to go all in and expect God to show up!

Looking at the children of Israel and where they were at, the idea of prosperity was so far removed from their reality, yet things changed with their first step of faith. God was demonstrating His heart for them by giving them what they deserved, worked for, desired and maybe dreamt of but had no access to. Grace at its fullness!

I remember being in a similar situation when I was leaving for the big unknown mission to United Kingdom. I had never travelled out of the country before but that was not my biggest challenge. My biggest challenge was that I lacked the necessary requirements that would enable me to leave. The call was there and strong, it seemed an impossible situation - how was it going to happen? I guess the Israelites might have been asking themselves the same question.

God directed me to go and speak to one of the senior minister in town who was on the same level of seniority in church hierarchy as the president. They happened to be friends and spent public time together. You can probably guess what my answer was – an outright NO!

I tried to do it my own way, and everything I tried didn't work and I started blaming those that promised to help. I got very desperate and in the end I decided to do it God's way begrudgingly! It wasn't about faith, fear had gripped me and I was scared because I viewed myself as unworthy and could not imagine what I was going to tell the great man of God!

I didn't see myself as God saw me, so the little insignificant me cowered away and hid; little did I know that was the beginning of many lessons on faith, trust and obedience!

God was going to teach me prosperity principles (albeit the hard way) that would not only transform my life but those of others.

I needed to trust Him wholly for like the children of Israel, I was entering the wilderness and was going to be tested, spiritually, mentally, physically, psychologically! My need for water, *manna*[iii], meat, training, and so much more was going to challenge everything I knew – it has been a faith boot camp!

The first step is to **trust that what you've asked for, you will receive**; this is one of the core prosperity principles that Jesus taught:

'And I say unto you, ***Ask, and it shall be given you****; seek, and you shall find; knock, and it shall be opened unto you'* (Luke 11:9).

Let's start asking with confidence and boldness believing it is given!

Giving and Receiving

There are different *ways* of giving, but I believe there are only two *types* of giving – conscious and unconscious. Most givers don't even know they are giving and therefore may not know if it's working for them or not. Those of us that come from large families especially if you have siblings and parents try to drum the concept of sharing in the system from an early age. What we don't understand is, sharing is giving as well.

The education system does attempt to teach children to share, sometimes not so successfully. This teaching by parents, school or extended family becomes our trained (subconscious) giving. We tend to do it out of obedience sometimes begrudgingly and can choose to either do or not based on feeling or circumstances.

However, I believe giving is an innate gift that is within each one of us, but somehow we lose it in our growing up experiences because the 'trained' giving overshadows it.

'I have showed you all things, how that so labouring you ought to support the weak, and to remember the words of the Lord Jesus, how he said, **It is more blessed to give than to receive**' *(Acts 20:35).*

The interesting thing about giving is this; it's a two-way street! Most people miss out on that when they quote the scripture above which has been overused. Giving is within us and in our nature as we are part of the Father. James tells us this:

'Every good and perfect gift is from above, coming down from the Father of the heavenly lights, who does not change like shifting shadows' **(James 1:17)**.

We are made in His likeness and, therefore, if He is a giver of good and perfect gifts, so are we. However, in our case, the 'trained' giving casts shifting shadows on our giving. It becomes conditional; hence it loses the meaning and the purpose of it.

God gives to us unconditionally, whether we deserve it or not. We breathe in air while awake or in our sleep and God never says, 'I am turning oxygen off on you because you've been ungrateful!' His unconditional love is not dependent on us; He continues to send us many good and perfect gifts regardless of our attitude.

Conscious giving is when you realise that giving and receiving are inseparable partners. They are not mutually exclusive; they always go together whether you know it or not. They are like night and day but you only see one at a time. That's why it's important to shift from the 'trained' to the 'conscious' giving for every time you give you are receiving though there may be a delay.

A way to illustrate it simply is this: for a farmer to get a harvest he must plant a seed – it is a law! If you found a farmer staring at an empty field angry that he didn't get a harvest, you would be confused. You will want to ask him questions: 'What did you plant? What happened to the seed?' And if he turns around and says he didn't plant anything, you will conclude there is an issue with his reasoning faculty.

In the example above, we understand very well but it's the same principle based on the following scripture:

> *'Don't be misled—you cannot mock the justice of God. **You will always harvest what you plant***' **(Galatians 6:7 NLT).**

This principle applies to everything and runs with other 'duality laws' that govern this universe that we live in. If you read the story of creation in the book of Genesis, you will see 'day and night,' 'light and darkness,' 'land and sea' and so on.

The most profound thing about these laws is that they work, whether you believe in God or not! To some people, this is shocking, and they would even argue the case. The truth brings freedom, and this book is about bringing the truth where money, God and you are concerned!

The world's richest women and men are **giving** billions of dollars to charities around the world! I have personally witnessed those large cheques being given to great social projects around the world and making a real difference to people's lives! Have you ever asked yourself why they give so much? Some people say they are avoiding paying high taxes but while the poor people are complaining and debating the *whys* and all that, the rich are busy sowing seeds and reaping the bumper harvest!

While we carry on with our view on this, let's revisit the parable Jesus taught in Matthew 25: 14 – 28 and I quote a part of it below:

> 'Then you should have deposited my money with the bankers, and on my return I would have received it back with interest. **Therefore take the talent from him and give it to the one who has ten talents. For everyone who has will be given more, and he will have an abundance.** But the one who does not have, even what he has will be taken away from him' (Matthew 25: 27 – 29 BSB).

Which merchant would you be?

There is a reasoning that goes like this, 'It is okay with the millionaires; they have plenty of money to give!' This robs many people of the blessing that comes with giving. They see themselves as disadvantaged forgetting, there are those entrusted with just the one talent. We are only called to be faithful with what we have been given.

God will never ask you to account for what He didn't give you! You are measured by what you have, not what you don't have! What did you do with it?

You see, I have been attending church for many years and over time I've heard many Christians, including myself, quote Apostle Paul to others:

'But my God shall supply all your need according to his riches in glory by Christ Jesus' (**Philippians 4:19**).

What is the context in which Philippians 4:19 above is written? Apostle Paul was giving this promise to a group of believers who were operating in God's principles of *giving and receiving, sowing and reaping* as discussed above.

When we quote this scripture we need to understand it's based on continuous giving and support the church at Philippi had given to Paul. If we go back to the law of sowing and reaping, sadly there are times when we are symbolically looking at an empty field and expecting a harvest. Shouldn't we sense-check ourselves before reeling scriptures at one another?

Paul was also reiterating Jesus' teaching that says:

> **'Give, and you will receive**. *Your gift will return to you in full - pressed down, shaken together to make room for more, running over, and poured into your lap. The* **amount you give will determine the amount you get back'** **(Luke 6:38 NLT).**

It is clear from Paul's letter that he loved the church at Philippi and had a very special relationship with them. Referring to his earlier ministry, he said: '*...no church but you partnered with me in the matter of giving and receiving'* **(Philippians 4:15 BSB).**

Paul's focus was on the harvest—for them to receive a harvest—when he said:

'I seek for the profit which increases to your account' **(Philippians 4:17 NASB).**

God is not a respecter of persons; as it rains on every land, so are these principles. If you follow them consciously, taking heed to *plant a seed*, He will meet all your needs according to His glorious riches in Christ Jesus, according to His word.

*'Remember this, a farmer who plants only a **few seeds will get a small crop**. But the one who plants **generously will get a generous crop**. You must each decide in your heart how much to give. And **don't give reluctantly or in response to pressure**. 'For God loves a person who gives cheerfully'* (2 Corinthians 9:6 - 7 NLT).

Tithing or Tenth (10%)

Have you ever given a tenth of your income to a cause you believe in?

*'**One tenth** of the produce of the land, whether grain from the fields or fruit from the trees, belongs to the LORD and must be set apart to him as holy'* (Leviticus 27:30 NLT).

This is the most common and most talked about form of giving within the Bible-believing community and most believers are familiar with the above text. Givers and non-givers all have an opinion on it – what it should or not be. Before we get into the technicality of tithing, let us look at its origins. I am about empowering you with facts concerning money and how it really works.

The first mention of 'tenth' as a gift or offering is mentioned in the book of Genesis.

Genesis 14 tells us of an uncle whose nephew gets in trouble, and he gets caught up in the mess, but something good does come out of it. I'm an Aunty and I have been caught up in my nieces' and nephews' messes, so I suppose it goes with the territory!

We meet a triumphant Abraham, he's just defeated the kings, but what follows is a story that is still partly mysterious today. A new character appears in his story, Melchizedek king of Salem:

*"After Abram returned from defeating Kedorlaomer and the kings allied with him, the king of Sodom came out to meet him in the Valley of Shaveh (that is, the King's Valley). Then **Melchizedek king of Salem** brought out bread and wine. **He was priest** of God Most High, **and he blessed Abram**, saying, 'blessed be Abram by God Most High, Creator of heaven and earth.*
*And praise be to God Most High, who delivered your enemies into your hand.' **Then Abram gave him a tenth of everything**"* (Genesis 14: 17-20 NIV).

The order of events here is important; the king of Sodom comes to meet Abraham but the person that brings him *'bread and wine'* is Melchizedek the priest. He comes out to bless Abraham with what we refer today as 'communion'; after which, he speaks a blessing to him! After the blessing, Abraham then gives Melchizedek a tenth of everything!

Note that the priest did not ask for anything but Abraham did what was natural to him – he blessed the priest right back. The law of giving and receiving is at play here, but not the usual 'you pay a compliment, so I pay you one', or 'you buy me a drink, so I owe you one' – not that type. Nowhere else are we told that Abraham and Melchizedek had met before or whether they were going to meet again.

This was conscious giving, the innate code that is in all of us. A verse after Abraham and Melchizedek had finished, the King of Sodom appeared on the scene and wanted to strike a deal with Abraham. Abraham recognised he was operating from a different place – trained giving (what's-in-it-for-me kind of giving).

"The king of Sodom said to Abram, 'Give me the people and keep the goods for yourself'" (Genesis 14:21).

Abraham was in the spirit; he had just encountered the source of his increase – Melchizedek, the King of

Salem[iv] – and he was not going to compromise, so he turned down the offer.

He had made an oath to the LORD that he would not accept anything from anyone, not even a *thread or the strap of a sandal,* lest they say *'I made Abraham rich!'* (Genesis 14:23).

After all, Abraham is on a mission to a vision! I love this man!

There is so much we can learn from this story and the order of things. Today, most people give their tithe because it is demanded of them and it is not from a cheerful heart. The modern day 'priest' is also demanding the tithe and so there is a conflict, and 'cheer' is taken out of it!

Apostle Paul says:

> *'You must each decide in your heart how much to give. And don't give reluctantly or in response to pressure. For God loves a person who gives cheerfully'* **(2 Corinthians 9:7 NLT)**.

Giving is a personal decision and should never be under duress, coerced or demanded! No vision or blessing will follow as in the case of Abraham, and you will quickly accept what the 'King of Sodom' has to offer. The characters in the story above are there for a reason! They represent the types of people we will meet on our faith journey. By knowing where your blessing comes from, you will be able to say no to what may seem like a good deal, albeit counterfeit.

Freedom to give cheerfully comes when you understand the laws that govern it. Melchizedek and Abraham demonstrated how it should be done. We know that Abraham did not lack in any way —he was one of the wealthiest patriarchs we know. He and his nephew Lot had to part company because they were so blessed and needed more space to continue to prosper!

From what we see above, a tithe is one-tenth of something given as a voluntary contribution to honour God. In my tribe, we don't have 'tithe' as a term. However, we have a phrase that we use, and there is not an English equivalent, but I have come to understand it was a tithe, even though it doesn't have a number. We say, *'give a hand back* for every act of kindness or deal, traditionally you would naturally give something back as a way of appreciation.' Sadly, the greedy people who don't understand its purpose have abused this great tradition.

Every time God blesses you, you would 'give a hand back' to say thank you to honour the Giver. Abraham accumulated great wealth through putting his faith in God and honouring Him by tithing.

The wise King Solomon wrote about 'giving a hand back' to God in the book of Proverbs.

> *'Honour the Lord with your possessions, And with the first fruits of all your increase; So your barns will be filled with plenty, And your vats will overflow with new wine'* (**Proverbs 3: 9-10 NKJV**).

There is no denying or running away from this fact: blessing and increase are synonymous with giving. What becomes questionable is how, why and to whom we give. Ignorant giving is like living a life of planting seeds and never going back for the harvest! Know your covenant rights and walk in them!

For many years I didn't understand this law applied to us all, believers and non-believers equally. It's a universal law that works irrespective of your faith!

Many years ago in Kenya, my friend Tony explained the law of giving to me and encouraged me to give my tithe. I still remember that conversation as if it were yesterday, though it's been over 20 years now. You see, I had a low paying job and I existed from payday to payday struggling to support my large family and myself.

None of what Tony said made any sense to me at the time. I didn't have much to give in the first place and therefore could not understand why God would want me to give from what I didn't have. Well, I reasoned that either way I didn't have much to lose since I was already struggling and if it worked I would be better off. I decided to give it a try. The unexpected happened and has continued to happen ever since! Somehow, my money seemed to have taken a new form, and from then on I seemed to have enough unlike before.

I like to test theories and concepts and can confirm I have tried this one over and over, it always comes back to me running over. In giving like everything else the heart attitude is very important. Giving is a personal decision that activates a law that let others see how it works!

*'Bring the entire tithe into the storehouse that there may be food in my house. So **put me to the test in this right now**,' says the LORD of the Heavenly Armies, 'and see if I won't throw open the windows of heaven for you and pour out on you blessing without measure.*

And I'll prevent the devourer from harming you, so that he does not destroy the crops of your land. Nor will the vines in your fields drop their fruit," says the LORD of the Heavenly Armies' (**Malachi 3:10-11 ISV**).

The same way you can't expect a harvest if you didn't plant anything is the same way you can't expect to receive if you didn't give – and if you do get, remember, it's a *debt*! I wish there were a way around this one, but I still haven't found it and I'm not even looking anymore! In my early days of giving, I have to honestly say I did have multiple conversations with me to convince myself about it. Forming any habit even the good ones is not easy; at the time I didn't have this knowledge and could not understand why I was struggling.

You will find that many modern-day believers expect to experience the same wealth Abraham experienced, yet struggle in the area of planting seeds. The argument that we are no longer under the Law of Moses but under grace is very valid; however, as we've seen above, tithing was there long before Moses!

If you want what Abraham had, then follow his blueprint; take time out and read **Galatians 3:6-29.**

There are many debates, views, opinions and even church policies on where to give your tithe, and therefore I believe it's important I include the text below. Let the Holy Spirit direct you.

*'Every third year you must offer a special tithe of your crops. In this year of the **special tithe** you must **give your tithes to the Levites, foreigners, orphans, and widows**, so that they will have enough to eat in your towns'* (Deuteronomy 26:12 NLT).

Plant Good Seeds

There is something mystic about the book of Ecclesiastes! It speaks in riddles, parables, emotions and one could easily miss the lessons with all the colour and drama contained in such a small book. The authorship of the book is accredited to King Solomon, although he is never named. It is said a teacher wrote it, the author whoever it is had a great deal of life experience and was talking from the heart. For clarity, going forward, I will refer to the author as 'The Teacher'.

The book runs the 'emotional scale' from totally depressed to being fully fulfilled, so there is much to learn from it, wherever you find yourself.

'There is nothing better for a person than that he should eat and drink and find enjoyment in his toil. This also, I saw, is from the hand of God' (Ecclesiastes 2:24 ESV).

Personally, I have learnt profound things from The Teacher, and at times I have also struggled to understand some of the text, because the meaning and purpose is not obvious; they raise questions that lead me on a quest for deeper understanding.

For the purpose of this book, we will look at the deep insight in the fundamental law of 'sowing' that God has set in place in the universe. It's coded in every living thing and where there is a blip in the system, the word 'extinct' is used in history.

Everything must produce after its own kind, and in order to achieve a harvest, a seed is required!

What does The Teacher in Ecclesiastes tell us about this fundamental law? What brings about **profit** (some translations use the word '***prosper***')?

> *'Plant your seed in the morning and keep busy all afternoon, for you don't know if **profit** will come from one activity or another - or maybe both'*
> **(Ecclesiastes 11:6 NLT).**

Do you limit yourself in any area of your life, and give a reason or a season why you can't do something? I have done that in the past many times, and sadly, family, school, friends, colleagues and the media all give us many reasons why we can't do things, and we buy those lies and live by them!

The big question is this: Who owns the reason you give to yourself and others? Where did it come from?

You are told you can't succeed if you don't have this level of education, this amount of money, family background, race, gender, culture and the list go on and on! The Teacher begs to differ and uses the farming background where there are so many set rules. He says, 'Don't limit yourself; break from the status quo and do what needs to be done regardless of the so-called conventional wisdom, for you do not know what will prosper.'

Let's look at it again!

'Plant your seed in the morning and keep busy all afternoon, for you don't know if profit will come from one activity or another - or maybe both'
(Ecclesiastes 11:6 (NLT).

This has been proven over and over; there are many inventions that would never have happened if the inventor would have given up after the first few times, but they kept going despite the discouragement. Thomas A. Edison is a classic example of extreme faith in an idea, a seed he believed so strongly that it was bound to succeed!

There are many people who sow one seed at a time and wait, and if it doesn't succeed, they are deeply disappointed, though I'm not sure with who; themselves or the seed.

I have quoted Ecclesiastes 11:6 (above) many times to myself in the past because I believe it to contain so much wisdom that is not necessarily obvious. The fact is this: time will pass whether you are sowing seeds or not so let us heed to wisdom that calls us to keep sowing seeds. That's the only way we are ever likely to get a harvest.

The knowing of whether the seed will succeed or not is in the planting!

Don't hold on to your seed, there is no increase in a well-guarded seed. Follow the words of Christ Jesus;

'Truly, truly, I say to you, unless a grain of wheat falls into the earth and dies, it remains alone; but if it dies, it bears much fruit' **(John 12:24 ESV)**.

But 'how do I sow my seed?' you may ask.

The Teacher continues with his advice in Ecclesiastes 11:2:

*'But divide your investments among many places,
for you do not know what risks might lie ahead'*
(Ecclesiastes 11:2 NLT).

The popular saying 'don't put all your eggs into one basket' comes to mind as I read above verse. This also applies to investing your money, any form of giving be it in tithes or offering. Wisdom calls you to open savings and investment accounts, give to charities, and help the poor and the needy in your community. Apply wisdom when you sow your seed, make sure the ground is fertile, reputable to give a good return for not every ground may be suitable.

The Teacher goes on to say:

'Cast your bread upon the waters, for you will find it after many days' **(Ecclesiastes 11:1 ESV).**

The Teacher does what every good teacher does; he uses repetition to make a point. Where do wealth and riches come from? They come from God, and he makes this point in almost every chapter! What are you supposed to do with the wealth, remain sad and miserable? No, you are meant to be joyful, have pleasure in what God has given you and not live in misery waiting for the life to come! God has set eternity *now* in your heart for a reason **(Ecclesiastes 3:11).**

Let me close this revealing chapter with these words from The Teacher:

'Furthermore, as for every man to whom God has given riches and wealth, He has also empowered him to eat from them and to receive his reward and rejoice in his labour; this is the gift of God' **(Ecclesiastes 5:19 NASB).**

In the next chapter we will identify and deal with money beliefs that are embedded in our *human Operating System™ (hOS™)*

CHAPTER 5

THE HUMAN OPERATING SYSTEM™ (hOS™)

*My people are destroyed for lack of **knowledge**: because thou hast rejected knowledge, I will also reject thee, that thou shalt be no priest to me: seeing thou hast forgotten the law of thy God, I will also forget thy children.* - **Hosea 4:6 (WBT)**

Beliefs

Today we are familiar with machine **operating systems (OS)** in our electronic devices like computers, tablets and smartphones. An OS is the core **system software** that manages device hardware and software resources and provides common services for the programmes to run.

Today the main OS for smartphones are either iOS, Android or Windows and while they have the same end result the machines perform differently based on the OS. Your OS will also determine what applications you have access to. The manufacturer determines the frequency of the software updates but it's up to the user when to install the updates. The reminders will be sent and will go on for a set period of time, and in the end, you the user will be forced to update the software!

Let's leave the *tech stuff* and just go on to relate the OS and software to the matter at hand. Do you know you too have an Operating System (OS)? This may or may not be a proven scientific fact, but it is a parallel illustration as to how the human system functions. Majority of us do not realise our lives are run on an automated operating system! In most people's case, there are many inputs to developing the 'software' of our life, which creates confusion, and lack of harmony!

Have you ever wondered what runs your life? Do you find yourself thinking about every little action or decision you make or are they mostly automatic? It's amazing to see how much computer technology has changed over the years, from a large monstrous machine kept in a special room, to many people carrying one around 24/7! I wonder how many of us, including myself, have seen a similar transformation in our beliefs and values in the same measure of time!

A few years back when I was learning about organisation cultures and what drives them, I came across a gentleman who had done a lot of research on this subject over a long period of time. I was so intrigued I ended up studying this subject beyond what was required. I found it touched on behaviours that I recognised about others and myself that went beyond the workplace. The greatest discovery for me was understanding how and when these beliefs were formed which is all about the hOS^{TM}. Information has the power to produce transformation!

According to *Gerard Hofstede*[v], a Dutch social psychologist and Professor Emeritus of Organisational Anthropology and International Management at Maastricht University in the Netherlands, our 'operating system' is formed and sealed by the age of 10.

He says, 'Values are among the first things children learn – not consciously, but implicitly. Development psychologists believe that **by the age of 10, most children have their basic value system**

firmly in place, and after that age, changes are difficult to make. Because they were acquired so early in life, many values remain unconscious to those who hold them. Therefore, they cannot be discussed, nor can they be directly observed by outsiders. They can only be inferred from the way people act under various circumstances.'

This information shocked me because, for the first time, I became aware of the little girl in me still making decisions based on her experiences as a child.

You might be surprised to hear that your relationship with money was born long before you can remember! While it might have been a conscious decision at the time, you might have been far too young to remember it.

In this chapter, we are going to look at the different doors that would have influenced your money belief system. Figure 1 (next page) attempts to explain the Complex Intelligent System™ you are. Over the years, you have collected and assimilated information from all the sources listed in the diagram. In the blink of an eye you analyse any given situation, and based on information stored in your brain from your sources and experiences you make a decision. It's almost instant, that's how good you are in recalling information! In actual fact, it's not really making a decision; it's the belief ('code') you have stored in your operating system that throws an answer. Imagine this, if it's out of date, then you will make an out-of-date decision that does not support you!

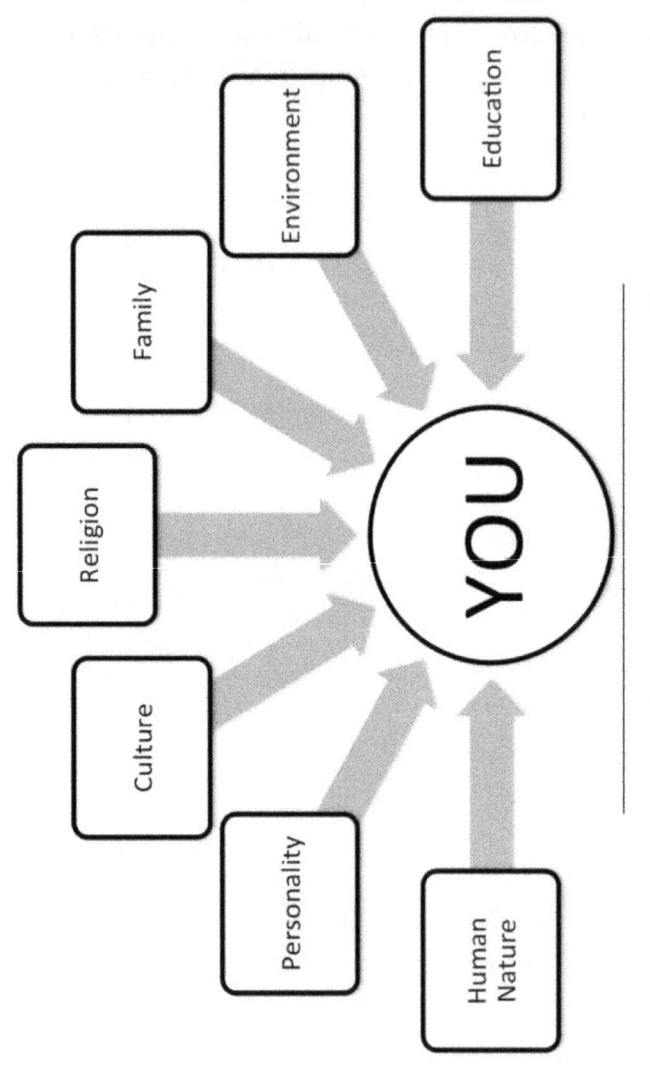

Figure 1. You – The Complex Intelligent System™

Culture

Culture: *the ideas, customs, and social behaviour of a particular people or society.*

'Culture' and 'custom' have the same meaning and when we study the Bible, we will see there were certain customs that were followed because they always were – you didn't question them. Christ Jesus upset the teachers of the day because He didn't seem to follow these customs.

"At about that time Jesus was walking through some grainfields on the Sabbath. His disciples were hungry, so they began breaking off some heads of grain and eating them.

But some Pharisees saw them do it and protested, 'Look, your disciples are breaking the law by harvesting grain on the Sabbath'" **(Matthew 12: 1- 2 NLT).**

The Pharisees had turned everything into laws to oppress people, and they did a great job of it. When you read the New Testament you will see the conflict between old and new culture is evident such that even those that walked side by side with Jesus struggled to break free from the old custom as we see in the book of Acts.

As we go through this section, it's important to ask several questions: What culture did I grow up in? What are the expected norms concerning money? Did you experience abundance or lack of wealth growing up? What was the reality of the people around you about wealth and money? How did your society view these individuals or families? If your culture viewed wealth as a negative thing, you will naturally have the same view embedded in your subconscious, as opinions and feelings towards the wealthy would have been passed down to you.

Reflect on your childhood, before age 10, and in your mind's eye see if you can identify wealth around you. What conversations about money do you remember? If you came from a wealthy family, what did others say about your family - your friends at school especially? It's interesting how children will want to give up what is good in their lives in order to fit with the norm!

I also believe that children view wealth differently, as their minds are not corrupted yet. This has changed over the years and continues to evolve as the internet has created easy access to global values mandated by popular culture.

It's important to understand that wealth is relative to your situation and also different cultures have different measures and definitions of wealth. While in some African cultures the size of livestock may have signified wealth, in the Western society, the make and model of a car or size of property may be the status symbol of wealth.

Looking back at my formative years I believed we were wealthy; however, by today's standard in the West where I live, we would be viewed as poor! What shaped your belief system is not how you see the past today but how you saw it then when you lived it – according to the social psychologist, before you were 10 years old!

I grew up with storytelling as an art; we competed with each other to see who could tell a story the best, adding drama and emotion to entertain or terrify one another. We were telling the folk tales passed down through generations, and the majority of them had deep meaning intricately weaved into the story. We learnt what was acceptable or not through these stories. As children we didn't realise the purpose of all the storytelling, it was just something we did to pass time as that was the evening entertainment available to us!

However, the basis for the storytelling, which was my cultural background, had already been faulted with cracks that would soon be showing. My tribe was among the first to be colonised in Kenya where I was born. As a third-generation child since adoption of Christianity, the many traditional cultural values began to lose hold and relevance because they were either 'educated or preached out' of the tribe as they were deemed barbaric by the colonial masters. While this is sad to read, each one of us must understand the fabric of the culture they grew up in and what influenced it.

So apart from the storytelling and its reduced effects, I grew up with a very western culture way of life, including learning English as the main education language and attending church regularly. I didn't complain about it because I didn't know any different, but the fact is it had its pros and cons. My relationship with money was formed from what I was taught in church and overhearing my parents talk about it on rare occasions it happened!

One important question to ask as an adult is this: Why was that belief important to my culture and my family, and where did it stem from? How has it served them, and how has it served me? This should be an honest object analysis for the result to be of value to you.

Bottom line, your cultural values concerning money may be deeply buried in your subconscious and you need to go back and ask yourself what they were and address them. They may be your big 'show stopper' and you are not even aware.

There are certain cultures that are labelled poor in the world and if you were born or raised in one of them, it's an uphill battle to free your mind from this trap. That's all it is, a mindset trap that can be removed.

At the beginning of this book, I made a claim that no one is born poor and I stand by it! Let's unlearn some rubbish!

Religion

> *'And you must love the LORD your God with all your heart, all your soul, all your mind, and all your strength'* **(Mark 12:30 NLT).**

I was introduced to church at an early age so when I use the term 'religion' as a source of one of our barriers to wealth I know what impact Christianity as a religion and philosophy has had on me where wealth is concerned.

I am intentionally using the term religion because regardless of the faith, all organised religions out there will teach on wealth. This book is principle-based and, therefore, not exclusive to Bible believers – like gravity, wealth has no favourites!

As a child with a limited vocabulary, everything can seem too complex and rather contradictory and so choosing the safer option in order to avoid trouble might be the better decision! For me, choosing to love the LORD with all my heart was what made sense and if money was going to keep me away from this resolve, then my choice was simple – I didn't want it.

What am I getting at, you may wonder? The verse below, the 10th Commandment, seems to contradict the desire for wealth and is thought to mean you can't have wealth as a believer. Most Bible translations use the term 'covet,' but below I chose a translation that uses 'desire.'

'Never desire to take your neighbour's household away from him. Never desire to take your neighbour's wife, his male or female slave, his ox, his donkey, or anything else that belongs to him' **(Exodus 20:17 God's Word Translation).**

Not to desire wealth? No! That is not the import of this scripture! The commandment here is not pointing to the wealth that God gives you; it is addressing lazy people who sit around eyeing their neighbour's stuff! This habit of desiring what the neighbour has will lead to many unkind things – jealousy, envy, bitterness, anger, greed, stealing, murder and all those other behaviours that will limit one from creating their own wealth as focus is misplaced!

When the commandment was given the Israelites had nothing to desire of one another. They were in the wilderness merely surviving. They needed a promise of a future that had abundance in it, where God was taking them – a 'land flowing with milk and honey'. God of hope wanted to start teaching them how to imagine the possibility of abundance when they got to the Promised Land. This is a characteristic of God helping people visualise what is possible in order to shift their focus from present circumstances, yet the children of Israel mourned and complained. They lived in the past longing for what they used to have, food like cucumbers, garlic, leeks, which made them want to quit and go back to the land of slavery. Living in the past will never help you move forward. The level of lack they were experiencing was affecting their belief system making them to become obsessed with assets – even other people's assets – and anything they could lay their hands on!

Apostle Paul wrote to the church in Philippi about being content with plenty and without it. To develop such mindset, you have to be confident in your Source. It's not about what your neighbour has; God has made sufficient provision for each of us. I mentioned earlier that conflict goes on in our minds when we receive two contradicting messages. The next scriptural text from the book of Luke is one that used to fill my mind with confusion; sadly it is used to prove by many that wealth is bad.

Now, before I even state the scripture here, as a child I could not understand the symbolism of putting a camel through the eye of a needle. I took it literally and saw it as practically impossible, yet I had the scripture repeated all the time!! It confused me for many years even as an adult due to my childhood take on it!

(Has this scripture ever tripped you? I would like to hear your thoughts on it serah@serahlister.com).

'It is easier for a camel to go through the eye of a needle than for a rich man to enter the Kingdom of God' **(Luke 18:25).**

The conversation between Christ Jesus and the young rich ruler was not about wealth but his true self and value system. If the young man was living according to Mark 12:30 (NLT), *'... love the LORD your God with all your heart, all your soul, all your mind, and all your strength'*, the conversation would have been different.

Elisha the prophet is a great example of living by Mark 12:30, he was a successful businessman who decided to give it all up and follow Elijah to fulfil the call of God.

God does not suffer insecurity and has no need to control you; he will never ask you to choose over Him or money! Our loving Father says;

'Come to me, all of you who are weary and carry heavy burdens, and I will give you rest. Take my yoke upon you. Let me teach you, because I am humble and gentle at heart, and you will find rest for your souls' (**Matthew 11: 28-28 NLT**).

Education

In most countries it is mandatory to get schooled, at home or in a physical school. There are many subjects that are taught and tested and it doesn't matter which country you are from, the differences as to how this is done are minimal.

For the purpose of this chapter we are going to focus on financial education. What type of education would you say the servant making the statement below had?

"The first servant reported, 'Master, I invested your money and made ten times the original amount!'" **(Luke 19:16 NLT).**

The language of money is alien to a lot of people, and the Bible teaches us in the book of Luke the importance of increase using the emotional language of money.

I was shocked to learn that in the United Kingdom, financial literacy education became part of the National Curriculum **for the first time** in September 2014 for children ages 11-16 years. One of the leading financial capitals of the world is not teaching its citizens about money! One would be forgiven for the cynicism of it all; so, was this intentional or did we just forget?

I grew up in Kenya; a country in Africa and for most people the only image they see in the media depicting Africa was of dying malnourished children! Africa and poverty were synonymous and maybe to some extent still is. You can see why not learning about financial literacy for me would be expected to some degree though not excusable! As for the U.K., I'm still trying to get my head around how something so important to success could have been off the curriculum!

Here's an opportunity for self-reflection; what was your financial education growing up? Were you taught financial literacy in school or through any other means? This is another moment to help identify where you picked up your moneymaking and management skills. Sometimes we believers can get so spiritual we are of no practical good to anyone even to ourselves! It is absolutely necessary that we learn to think and take action while seeking God at the same time.

Here's an example of what I'm talking about: While still writing this book, I heard of a lady who testified in church that she had been offered a business opportunity, but she turned it down because she didn't want it to keep her from God! Personally, I don't understand the reasoning behind her decision so will leave it at that but this is an example of how we can over-spiritualise money matters.

I applaud U.K.'s decision in 2014 to teach financial literacy in schools for children ages 11-16 years. However, I question whether we are not starting too late and missing out on the opportunity to cement these fundamentals as beliefs. Again, Gerard Hofstede, the Dutch social psychologist, believes that ***by the age of 10, most children have their basic value system firmly in place, and after that age, changes are difficult to make.***

While it's great that financial literacy is being taught in schools in the U.K. to children age 11+, we need to start teaching this important subject a lot earlier than that, and not just in the U.K. alone but universally. A global movement is necessary to empower generations financially and need to start *now* if we are to be free from the poverty mentality!

I remember when my son was in primary school and the children in his class were asked to bring old toys they didn't need to sell in aid of raising money for charity. He got so excited about it, every day he would raid his toy box and come home happy because he'd sold them albeit for 20 to 50 pence each! It all changed one morning when I saw a toy that had originally cost over £20 sitting on the table ready to become 50p merchandise!

It was at the moment I realised that, selling these toys was a game that gave him the thrill every good salesman experiences! Money meant nothing to him at this point.

Mama had to intervene; there were fundamental money lessons he needed to learn. I took him to the shop and explained the basics of buying, and selling at profit. We walked around the shop identifying what he could buy and sell at 20 pence while still making a profit. Simple but important lessons provided by the school project that I could have easily missed!

'My people are destroyed for lack of knowledge. Because you have rejected knowledge, I also will reject you from being My priest' **(Hosea 4:6a NASB).**

The text above was quoted previously in Chapter 2 of this book (under the subhead,

Stop the Money and Mammon Talk!*)* and my son's school project demonstrates how lack of knowledge can lead us astray. Not that we don't want to do what is right, sometimes it's simply because we don't know any different. Contrary to common belief, what you don't know can kill you and it's actually worse than what you know because you can't take any action! It's easy to address what you know; on the other hand you have no chance of rectifying something you are not aware of. You hear in press statements 'silent killer' or 'ticking time-bomb' when experts believe there is an underlying undetected problem in the society.

Financial illiteracy is one of the 'silent killers' in our society today! Large debts in just about every household and so many people leave university with big loans. The education system is set that way and this loan system is perceived as normal and encouraged leaving many people blindly enslaved to the financial institutions.

How about teaching our youngsters how to save and manage money well before then! There is a hypothesis out there that low financial literacy scores among young people is due to lack of motivation. Really? I disagree with that hypothesis completely - how can you get motivated to achieve high scores on something that you are not informed in?

The old mindset that 'you only need to learn about money if you work in the financial industry' is wrong and misleading. We all deal with money on a day-to-day basis, and there is no avoiding it if you are on planet earth!

The scripture below taken from the book of Proverbs tells us that iron sharpens iron, and clearly one cannot teach that which they don't understand. For most of us, what we learn in the education system forms the foundation of what we know about any given subject. Money is not a subject in isolation, and we are passing down zero financial literacy to those believers we continue to teach about giving -- that is only part of the equation.

'As iron sharpens iron, so one person sharpens another' **(Proverbs 27:17 NIV).**

This may get some people defensive, if not offended; however, I don't remember being taught the moneymaking and managing principles in my many years in the church. I hope this has not been your experience. The teaching we hear in the majority of churches are not about making, saving or managing money, but giving money!

To be clear, this book is not about giving an offering or tithe, but a wake-up call for you to take the time to understand and sort out your relationship with money!

God wants you to prosper!

Rebirth

'Do not be conformed to this world, but be transformed by the renewing of your mind. Then

you will be able to discern what is the good, pleasing, and perfect will of Go' (**Romans 12:2 BSB**).

Wherever you find yourself, remember, all is not lost! God has a consistent habit of always throwing us a lifeline! Maybe you've gone through this chapter and felt a little bit discouraged and may be wondering, 'How can I get out of here?' It was important for me to state the root of the problem; otherwise, like the Pharisees, it's easy to 'clean the cup on the outside' while all dirt and grime are hidden inside. Christ Jesus called them 'whitewashed tombstones' for a good reason!

Money misconceptions start very early in our childhood, and many people don't even know they have these ingrained beliefs. Some have accepted they are not meant to prosper and have been given a good reason for it. Living in denial of the truth that God wants you to prosper! No one can make you do anything you don't want; we only do that which makes sense to us.

Here's a translation of grandmother's saying – *'You can take a cow to the river, but you can't make it drink!'*

If you are reading this book I want to believe you are not one of those people content with poverty, for they would never agree with the principles in this book. There is enough information here to challenge anyone that lacks understanding in financial matters, address the root beliefs concerning money and uproot them!

Apostle Paul stated that we can be transformed in every area of our lives. That transformation comes by the **renewing of the mind**! Knowing who you are in Christ Jesus, what you are entitled to, confessing it and walking in it!

This will not be an overnight process as it has taken a long time to ingrain those unsupportive money principles learnt along the way, and maybe some through painful life experiences. There will be internal emotional battles as well, so it will take commitment on your side to undo. What you think God says about abundance and money is your key to receiving it, remember **all things are possible** to those who are in Christ Jesus! *Your belief is your faith; your faith is your reality.*

"Jesus looked at them intently and said, 'Humanly speaking, it is impossible. But not with God. Everything is possible with God'" **(Mark 10:27 NLT).**

Those unsupportive values and beliefs concerning God and money if not confronted will comfortably live in you unchallenged until kingdom come, and you may never know why you never prosper even with all the hard work! Friend, it is time to allow God to do a new thing in your life, forgetting what is behind. Let God make fertile your financial desert through the principles in this book, let him bless and give you increase in the work of your hands to pass on an inheritance to generations to come!

'Do not remember the past events, pay no attention to things of old. Look, I am about to do something new; even now it is coming. Do you not see it? Indeed, I will make a way in the wilderness, rivers in the desert' **(Isaiah 43: 18-19 HCSB).**

CHAPTER 6

RESPECT THE BUSINESS OF GOD

Delight yourself in the LORD, and he will give you the desires of your heart.

—Psalm 37:4 (ESV)

Jehovah Jireh

One of the major problems most religious people have with wealth and money is that they see it completely removed from their relationship with God. It's similar to the way we look at these two natural elements that can never mix naturally – oil and water.

Our God is Jehovah Elohim; He has many attributes and one of His names is **Jehovah Jireh** first mentioned in Genesis 22. It is mentioned for the first time at the end of a very dramatic story that takes place between God, a father, and his son!

A profound story of love, faith, trust and unity. Isaac (the son) trusted the father, Abraham who, in turn, trusted God. Isaac trusted the father enough not to have all the details, and Abraham trusted God enough to venture out into unknown believing God knows all! It challenges me every time I look at it; from every angle I ask myself whether I have that level of faith in God!

If you truly believe that God is who He says He is, then you never have to have all the details upfront and by faith you can experience His fullness and presence in your life without letting yourself get in your own way!

Let's look at part of the conversation between father and son:

> *"But Isaac spoke to Abraham his father and said, 'My father!'*
> *And he (father) said, 'Here I am, my son.'*
> *Then he (son) said, 'Look, the fire and the wood, but where is the lamb for a burnt offering?'*
>
> *And Abraham said, 'My son, God will provide for Himself the lamb for a burnt offering.' So the two of them went together"* (Genesis 22:7-8 NOG - GW).

Abraham displayed faith from the beginning; what do you tell the child you are about to go and sacrifice? Many parents are faced with that awkward moment when the child asks you a question about something you'd rather not tell them; do you tell them the whole truth or are you economical with the truth? Parenting 101!

I will not write the full story here but suggest you read Genesis 22 to fill in the gaps. Abraham and Isaac get to their destination, and there the truth was revealed; Isaac was the sacrifice.

While today this sounds like a practice of the occult and many people might see it as a reason not to believe in a God demanding human sacrifice, for me, the lessons for us are clearly woven into the story. Here was a man who had such faith in God that he would go to great lengths of self-surrender because of trust. This trust allowed Abraham to discover this powerful attribute of God – **Jehovah Jireh**!

'When Abraham looked around, he saw a ram behind him caught by its horns in a bush. So Abraham took the ram and sacrificed it as a burnt offering in place of his son. Abraham named that place **Yahweh Yireh'** (Genesis 22:13-14 NOG - GW).

The following words in the book of Samuel remind us to trust, respect, and have faith in God's ability in the face of challenges; *to obey is better than sacrifice*. Like Abraham, the journey to wealth and prosperity should start with trusting God in what he says concerning you! His will is that you may prosper.

Walking with God requires faith and absolute trust; the words in 1 Samuel 15:22 (below) spoken to King Saul, are a reminder of our relationship with God and what's important:

'Then Samuel said: Does the LORD take pleasure in burnt offerings and sacrifices as much as in obeying the LORD? Look: **to obey is better than sacrifice**, *to pay attention is better than the fat of rams'* (1 Samuel 15:22 HCSB).

Your wealth is God's business and requires faith in God; one must first believe that *'it is He who gives you the power to make wealth'* and not just when you have it. He is our everlasting provider, Jehovah Jireh!

True Humility and Defeating Fear

Humility is one of those attributes that is difficult to quantify, but is of great value to relationships. You will hear statements like 'someone lacks humility' or 'they are humble', which raises a concern in my mind because without supporting examples these are just words. What is the measure of humility?

On the other hand, biblical humility does not carry the same meaning as the word humility in today's language. Sadly, because of the biblical requirement or the use of the quality 'humility,' there are many people who confuse it with being a doormat, unimportant, weak, poor, never speaking up and the like.

Truth be told, outward appearance and use of language does not demonstrate humility and could equate to a false type. That is not biblical humility but a counterfeit of what the Bible talks about. True humility is deeper than the five known senses and has no desire in comparing itself with others.

Let's look at a text from the book of Luke in the New Testament.

> *"Two men went to the Temple to pray. One was a Pharisee, and the other was a despised tax collector. The Pharisee stood by himself and prayed this prayer: 'I thank you, God, that I am not a sinner like everyone else. For I don't cheat, I don't sin, and I don't commit adultery. I'm certainly not like that tax collector'"* **(Luke 18:9-14 NLT)**

The type of humility demonstrated in the text above by the Pharisee is self-seeking, external and mainly used for self promotion, righteousness and gain. True humility comes from the heart and is totally dependent on God for everything.

Let's look at another verse:

*'True humility and **fear** of the LORD lead to riches, honor, and long life'* **(Proverbs 22:4 NLT)**.

Many times over in the Bible, you will see the words 'humility' and 'fear of the Lord' together, but what does fear of the Lord mean?

Many have lived in 'great fear of the Lord' because they don't want to be struck by thunder or fire from heaven! I suppose that's where I started and soon realised from my own experience that there was something wrong with this type of doctrine.

Let me share a very personal story. I loved my late father very much; he was my role model, but there was a big problem! I could only love him secretly because I was afraid of him and, therefore, didn't trust him. The issue of trust separated us even though it seemed unfounded as my father had never caned me, which he did regularly to my siblings especially my brothers. What I observed was enough for me to stay on guard for it traumatised me terribly even though he never touched me. I was daddy's little girl spoilt in every way yet I was scared of him so much that I could not enjoy this privilege!

Let me demonstrate the impact that father-daughter relationship had on me in later life. When I came into a relationship with God as Father, I brought the model of the relationship I had with my father with me. Hearing Bible texts about 'fear the Lord' reinforced the fear I already held from my childhood.

How was I ever going to get all the promises spoken about me in the Bible if I couldn't trust Father God?

It is easy to love someone from afar with words spoken or written but what use is it? Trust bridges distance to connect us with love! *Fear destroys trust.*

So, what is this 'FEAR the Lord' that believers quote over and over, especially from the Old Testament text? My understanding and translation of it is *'reverence'*, awe, a state of heart and mind in worship and adoration. Let us compare the text in the book of Hebrews using different translations:

> *'Therefore, since we are receiving an unshakable kingdom, let us be filled with gratitude, and so worship God acceptably with* **reverence** *and awe'* **(Hebrews 12:28 BSB).**

> *'Since we are receiving a kingdom that is unshakable, let us be thankful and please God by worshiping him with* **holy fear** *and awe'* **(Hebrews 12:28 NLT).**

I'm yet to understand and be able to distinguish between general fear and 'holy fear.' If you can fear and trust at the same time, that is a great achievement and we would like to learn from you! If you have been able to do this, do write to me.

'Blessed is the man who is **in awe of Lord Jehovah** and takes heed to his commandments. **His seed shall be mighty** in the Earth and he will be blessed in the generation of the righteous ones. **Possessions and riches will increase in his house** and his righteousness will abide for eternity' **(Psalm 112:1-3 Aramaic Bible in Plain English).**

I love the above translation; it makes me want to dance in delight, for fear is not to be found in the verse at all. Interestingly, back in the day when I came to the realisation that 'fear' didn't represent what I believed it to mean, I didn't have access to as many Bible translations and commentaries as I have today and I am glad for the technological era of open access we are in!

If this is the first time you are encountering this difference in translation, take time to look up these verses in different translations of the Bible, they are freely available on the Internet.

Become A Money Magnet

There's one thing I'm going to say before I write anything about King Solomon and the book of Proverbs. It blows my mind that with all the bad rap being wealthy gets, the best down-to-earth advice for godly living comes from a man who had more wealth than can be described! Let that be at the back of your mind as we go through this section.

One consistent thing we get from the authors of the book of Proverbs is this: you must be grounded in wisdom at all times! Another one of those fundamental life principles: no matter who, what, where, when, how and everything else, ***find wisdom***! *This is the key to life!*

King Solomon summarises it for us in the following text:

> 'Happy is the person who finds wisdom. And happy is the person who gets understanding.
>
> Wisdom is worth more than silver. It brings more profit than gold. Wisdom is more precious than rubies. Nothing you want is equal to it.
>
> With her right hand wisdom offers you a long life. With her left hand she gives you riches and honor'
>
> **(Proverbs 3:13-16 International Children's Bible ICB).**

Sadly, there are many people who read the verses above and believe that wisdom is all you are meant to get and that's it. Wisdom is the beginning, where you start the journey. Wisdom is active; it will activate your faith and start bearing fruit in your life. As we read in the above text, with the right hand wisdom *offers* you *long life*, and with the left it *gives* you *riches*! Notice, one aspect is offered while the other is given.

Further in the book of Proverbs, we find the text below:

'For whoever finds me finds life, and shall obtain favour of the LORD' **(Proverbs 8:35 AKJV).**

While there is still a debate among Bible scholars as to who or what wisdom is, my personal belief is that wisdom as spoken of in the Bible refers to the Holy Spirit who had not been revealed (as we know Him today) in the days of King Solomon. Wisdom was there before beginning of time, still is and forever will be!

I remember, many years ago, a visiting preacher brought the significance of the scripture below to my attention. Painfully I learnt I needed to prosper. It was not just so I could have a comfortable life, but I needed to be a good steward too and leave an inheritance, not only to my child but my grandchildren too! You can't leave an inheritance of wealth that you don't have; I realised I had to find a way to prosper! I had to change my thinking for God does not contradict Himself.

> *'A good person leaves an inheritance to his grandchildren'* **(Proverbs 13:22a ISV)**.

I have to admit sometimes knowing something puts one under pressure because it takes away the excuses of not knowing. There are times I find myself battling with it, but it's always better to be in the know than be banging your head in the dark!

There is a relationship between wisdom and riches; as I mentioned earlier, wisdom is active and won't sit still. It has to produce fruits after its own kind.

> *'The crown of the wise is their riches: but the foolishness of fools is folly'* **(Proverbs 14:24)**.

There is no room for idleness in King Solomon's world, and honestly, laziness does bring poverty with it. I recently had a conversation with someone who loves to defend the poverty stand and regardless of what the scriptures say, he will not accept another way! He gave reason after reason why some people should be poor and find scripture to support this position.

What are your views; does God want some people to be poor?

'Take a lesson from the ants, you lazybones. Learn from their ways and become wise! Though they have no prince or governor or ruler to make them work, they labour hard all summer, gathering food for the winter' **(Proverbs 6:6-8 NLT).**

We all have bad habits and one of mine was to hit the snooze button in the morning and say, 'I'm not a morning person,' but when the words in Proverbs 24:33 come to mind I remember laziness comes with 'a little slumber' and quickly get out of bed!

King Solomon achieved so much, and left a legacy we still talk about today. He invented the hanging gardens, sewer system, and many more inventions! It is true he inherited a wealthy kingdom from his father, but he didn't sit idle as one would expect but he continued to work hard to build his own legacy.

'A little extra sleep, a little more slumber, a little folding of the hands to rest then poverty will

pounce on you like a bandit; scarcity will attack you like an armed robber' Proverbs 24:33-34 ESV)

Some of the principles and scriptures in this book will challenge your doctrine, philosophy and belief where wealth is concerned; however, if you are seeking to prosper, then you must be willing to allow these words to take root and bear fruit in you.

I admit to this: I am the queen of long drawn conversations and debates with God; taking *'come let's reason together'* text in Isaiah 1 literally! I like to talk matters over with God in a deep and philosophical manner asking questions and giving my perspective and worldview of the situation. Has such attitude paid off for me? Yes, it has!

Generosity versus Greed

Wealth is not one-sided; it's not just about what you can have, as that would create an imbalance in the perfectly balanced universe. Malachi Chapter 3 refers to this kind of greed and calls it robbing God.

Greed or the need to abuse what is rightfully deserved and take advantage of others is a prevalent human problem in the world going back in time. Most countries have labour laws to ensure that we value and honour each other, so people are not abused and taken advantage of for any service provided.

Long before that, God put principles in place to take care of this type of human behaviour. Take these principles as the universal labour laws that enforce themselves, they work whether one believes in them or not!

In the book of Luke, we see the instruction Christ Jesus gave His disciples when He sent them out to preach the Good News. They were not to carry provisions with them; they were to be provided for where they were received, and in return, they would leave a blessing. If a house or a city did not receive them, then no blessing would be left. As you can see, even where there is no pre-agreed contract a receipt of service demands a form or reward.

> *'Remain in the same house, eating and drinking what they offer, for the worker is worthy of his wages. Don't be moving from house to house'* (Luke 10:7 HCSB).

What most people don't realise (and neither did I until I came in contact with contract law), is that by merely accepting services from a person or company, you have entered into an agreement with them! This was eye opening for me. By law, it doesn't matter whether you signed a contract or not; as long as you received a service, the law will force you to pay for it.

The courts are merely enforcing a spiritual law, and that's why we as believers need to understand this book we call the Bible, for it is full of wisdom – I call it God's goldmine!

What gets in the way is greed; we go as far as withholding from God as we have the free-will to do as we choose. The truth sets us free, even with free-will this spiritual law is self-enforced and unbeknown to us we blindly suffer the consequencies.

Again, below we see Apostle Paul labouring on the point, bringing scriptures from the Old Testament to emphasise his point. There is no avoiding the issue of greed and withholding wealth; we must *'give Caesar what belongs to Caesar'* as Christ Jesus put it!

> *"Those Elders who lead well deserve double honour, especially those who toil in the word and in teaching. For the Scriptures say,* **'Do not muzzle the ox while it is treading,'** *and,* **'The labourer deserves his wages'"** (1 Timothy 5:17 -18 **Aramaic Bible in Plain English**).

If we can take the time to get into the flow of the Bible, it becomes very clear that there is always a good reason and a *benefit* to everything that is required of us. Christ Jesus illustrated this point in His teaching in Luke 6, reminding us that it is not all in vain.

'Give, and it shall be given unto you; good measure, pressed down, and shaken together, and running over, shall men give into your bosom. For with the same measure that you use, it will be measured back to you' (Luke 6:38).

Apostle Paul reinforces what Christ Jesus taught as recorded in the book of Luke making the same point. The Bible uses repetition to emphasise a point yet we still struggle to grasp the message! Maybe you are different but I know for me, even after many years of reading the Bible through, I am blown away by the many revelations I get from the same text I have read 20 times! How is that?

The Bible is a book full of spiritual principles, and they must be spiritually discerned; as so, we are on a journey and will continue to learn more as we evolve with the word. 'It can't be, I read it once and it didn't work for me' attitude; no book or philosophy is like that - you need to soak yourself in and become one with the contents of the book!

*'Remember this, a farmer who plants only a few seeds will get a small crop. But the one who plants generously will get a generous crop. You must each decide in your heart how much to give. And **don't give reluctantly or in response to pressure**. For God loves a person who gives cheerfully'* **(2 Corinthians 9:6 - 7 NLT).**

The heart attitude comes into everything we do or say; no one can see that aspect of us but God, who is the one who rewards us from His storehouse. It doesn't matter what anyone thinks or says, go with the heart - it knows the language of God!

CHAPTER 7

THE FRUITS OF LAW AND GRACE

Therefore, since we have been made right in God's sight by faith, we have peace with God because of what Jesus Christ our Lord has done for us. Because of our faith, Christ has brought us into this place of undeserved privilege where we now stand, and we confidently and joyfully look forward to sharing God's glory.
—**Romans 5:1-2 (NLT)**

Justified

Two of the most powerful tools of oppression and control are guilt and shame; they have the power to conquer and rule the mind! They don't need monitoring; they do a perfect silent job to oppress the person who welcomes them into their mind. They are difficult to silence or uproot. There are many believers who live in a constant state of 'sin' guilt, never being good enough to please God! Every time they do something, they have a conversation with guilt and shame, and, sadly, these two will always answer yes—you are guilty as you charge yourself.

This is not a new phenomenon and Apostle Paul had to address this struggle with indwelling sin. The believers of his day had come from a background of faith by rules; they had to constantly go and offer sacrifice for the washing of their sins. To take the place of bulls, Christ Jesus came to atone for our sins so we don't have to offer sacrifices anymore. He did it once and for all but old habits die hard. The new believers in Christ Jesus had real struggles with the inner man who did not understand grace and wanted to observe the old law for atonement. What was born out of that inner conflict was condemnation and Apostle Paul, in his teachings, got to the heart of the matter:

'*Therefore there is now no condemnation, no guilty verdict,* *no punishment for those who are in Christ Jesus who believe in Him as their personal*

*Lord and Saviour. For **the law of the Spirit of life** which is in Christ Jesus, the law of our new being **has set you free from the law of sin and of death**.*

*For **what the Law could not do** that is, overcome sin and remove its penalty, its power being weakened by the flesh man's nature without the Holy Spirit, God did: He sent His own Son in the likeness of sinful man as an offering for sin.*

And He condemned sin in the flesh subdued it and overcame it in the person of His own Son, so that the righteous and just requirement of the Law might be fulfilled in us who do not live our lives in the ways of the flesh guided by worldliness and our sinful nature, but live our lives in the ways of the Spirit guided by His power' **(Romans 8:1-4 AMP).**

There is a huge difference between your conscience or that inner guidance telling you where you have gone wrong, to living under guilt and shame. It is important to know the difference, and the Holy Spirit[vi] keeps us in check and speaks to us through our inner voice.

Religiosity!

Would you ever openly admit you are a religious robot? You've been saying all the right things while your subconscious beliefs are sabotaging you!

The subconscious mind rules most times as that's where your values and beliefs are safely stored away and runs the show without you being aware. Matters of faith are not exempt from this pre-programmed super machine. I have learnt from my own experience that I need to dig deep to make my subconscious mind conscious if I am to grow in my faith.

My faith programme runs deep and goes back to my childhood when, as a child, I attended Sunday School where I memorised Bible verses, chapters, and songs that meant nothing to me since my vocabulary was very limited. The truth is this: I stored every single one of them and I can still quote them to you today at least with some understanding. What impact did they have on my value system? What about you, when did you come into contact with the Bible or Bible teachers?

'Therefore, there is now no condemnation for those who are in Christ Jesus, because through Christ

Jesus the law of the Spirit who gives life has set you free from the law of sin and death' **(Romans 8: 1-2).**

I have quoted the verse above many times but, honestly, it was something I had memorised, it sounded good but I never really looked at it analytically to get deep understanding for myself. According to the author, there are two laws at work—the 'law of the spirit' (grace) and the 'laws of sin and death' (Law). In grace, there is no condemnation, while on the other hand, the law condemns. They seem to be in conflict; there is a thin line, and if by any chance you come from a background of legalistic teachings, then your subconscious could still be tricking you.

What you come into contact with first will always try and rule and create a stronghold! Apostle Paul struggled with this, by his own confession, he was a master in practising the law; he was born into it and taught it as well, as you can see in the text below:

'I was circumcised when I was eight days old. I am a pure-blooded citizen of Israel and a member of the tribe of Benjamin--a real Hebrew if there ever was one! I was a member of the Pharisees, who demand the strictest obedience to the Jewish law' **(Philippians 3:5 NLT).**

I had not given the subject of 'law' and 'grace' much thought, as I believed I walked in grace, singing to others and myself that it was by grace that I had been saved. The reality is that saying, doing, and living are very different activities, and waking up to this simple reality was a slap in the face and true faith awakening. I was saying and believing I was living the grace life; however, on reflection, I had so many rules around my faith; the list of dos and don'ts determined what I did and how I felt. I was riddled with guilt and shame, for the *'do nots'* seemed to outweigh the *dos* by far in my life!

This is what Apostle Paul said about his struggle with the law:

'I don't really understand myself, for I want to do what is right, but I don't do it. Instead, I do what I hate' **(Romans 7:15 NLT)**.

This confession from Apostle Paul reminds me that I am not alone in this struggle and there is a victory if we persevere.

My early interaction with God was very legalistic, and believed His love was dependent on how good I was! I struggled to pray and relate because I would always remember what I did wrong, and after confessing that one, then another one came up. I would never be good enough to approach God 'with boldness and confidence' or to call him Abba Father because I felt guilty all the time. Yet the text below reminds me that I received love while I didn't even recognise or acknowledge the giver.

What foolishness (in Apostle Paul's words to the Galatians) bewitched me to think I needed to earn that love?

'God proves His love for us in this: While we were still sinners, Christ died for us' (**Romans 5:8 BSB**).

If you have found yourself struggling in an area of your life, I hope you can breathe a sigh of relief as you read this. Over the years in my faith walk, I have had many conversations with people from around the world who live in fear of not being good enough, with judgment and accusing voice haunting them. The wrath of God paralyses them to the point that they don't even know how to relate with Him to receive His unconditional love that He has shed in our hearts.

With my personal experience, I have attempted to paint a picture of this loving Father God who loves unconditionally to such people but they still struggle to relate with Him in that capacity. If you live by the law, you will struggle to fully trust the love of God, that undeserved favour that has nothing to do with your works. This is what He says to you;

> *'I have swept away your sins like a cloud. I have scattered your offenses like the morning mist. Oh, return to me, for I have paid the price to set you free'* **(Isaiah 44:22 NLT).**

Moses handed down the Law or 'the letter', while Grace came through Christ Jesus. It is important to understand that I'm not in any way advocating we do away with the Old Testament, but standing on what Jesus said; *'He didn't come to destroy the law, but He came to fulfil it'*. He fulfilled the demands of the law for us by becoming a curse in our place.

> *"Christ redeemed us from the curse of the law by becoming a curse for us, for it is written: 'Cursed is everyone who is hung on a pole'"* **(Galatians 3:13).**

God the Father wants to have a relationship with you; He intended this from the beginning, and He has made a way.

> *'For it is by grace you have been saved through faith, and this not from yourselves; it is the gift of*

God, not by works, so that no one can boast'
(Ephesians 2:8-9 BSB).

But how does grace measure against the law?

Bondage or Freedom

Bondage, as a word, brings to mind many bad and painful images, and there is nothing positive about it. It speaks of oppression, captivity, slavery, chains, control and many more negative experiences.

On the other hand, freedom speaks for itself; the two words are like night and day.

I believe from the depth of my heart that where the Spirit of the Lord is, there is freedom and Christ Jesus is the ultimate example of that freedom!

This freedom is so extreme it could be abused, and Apostle Paul made this clear:

'For the Lord is the Spirit, and wherever the Spirit of the Lord is, there is freedom' **(2 Corinthians 3:17 NLT).**

You need the wisdom to know what is beneficial to you, otherwise you could abuse the freedom, and I have seen it done by lovely brothers and sisters.

When you find yourself caught up in the dos and don'ts, there is no freedom at all, as your rule book determines your actions. The sad thing is the rulebook we live by has been passed down from previous generations. Many believers say it's in the Bible however; they will struggle to show you exactly where it is or tell you why it is observed. Be guided by the Holy Spirit, use discernment, take responsibility and know the word of God for yourself.

The following text from Paul's letter to the Corinthians touches on the difference between law and grace and the freedom grace brings. Grace gives you the confidence to approach God, to call yourself a child of God, a competent minister of the new covenant! The old false humility, 'I'm-not-worthy attitude' has no place in grace; we should walk confidently by grace!

> *'Such **confidence** we have through Christ before God. Not that we are competent in ourselves to claim anything for ourselves, but our competence comes from God. He has made us competent as ministers of a new covenant – **not of the letter***

but of the Spirit; for the letter kills, but the Spirit gives life' (2 Corinthians 3:4-6).

Apostle Paul's letter to the Romans lays a further claim to this freedom; we have been released, and we know there is no release without first bondage. Apostle Paul says we have been released from the law that had us bound! Now we live and serve in a new way, the way of grace.

'But now, having died to what bound us, we have been released from the Law, so that we serve in the new way of the Spirit, and not in the old way of the written code' (Romans 7:6).

Sadly, as we know from historical facts, the masters of bondage don't like to let go, even after a release has been declared. A struggle ensues between the master and the freed being. Sadly, once they are freed, they also struggle with their newfound freedom because there are no set rules to live by. They feel lost and end up creating new rules, so end up putting themselves back in bondage.

Looking as far back as the early church, there are many believers who have created new laws for themselves, bringing bondage as a result, forgetting Christ Jesus stands for freedom. We are reminded not to let ourselves be tied up again by the slavery of the law!

'It is for freedom that Christ has set us free. Stand firm, then, and do not let yourselves be burdened again by a yoke of slavery' **Galatians 5:1 (NIV).**

It is time to break loose from those chains and start enjoying the freedom that Christ Jesus brought you! If you are suffering from guilt and shame, there is a possibility that you have allowed the *'accuser of the brethren' (Revelations 12:10)* to come and whisper lies to you.

Christ Jesus came to bring you freedom; He paid the ultimate price for it. You are free indeed and no matter what lies about yourself you hear in your head, remember, the father of lies also known as the accuser of the brethren is not interested in your freedom.

Ask the Holy Spirit, our teacher, to instruct you and give you boldness and confidence to stand your ground as a child of God!

Scarcity or Abundance

Let me start this section with a quote from the late Stephen Covey:

'Most people are deeply scripted in what I call the Scarcity Mentality. They see life as having only so much, as though there were only one pie out there. And if someone were to get a big piece of the pie, it would mean less for everybody else.' – **Stephen Covey, The 7 Habits of Highly Effective People**, 1990 [vii]

While this may seem out of place here, scarcity is born of a limiting belief that says there is only so much available, therefore setting a limit to what is accessible.

The truth is this, there is no scarcity in God and I hope to demonstrate why in this section. When you look at creation, everything was made to keep producing 'after its own kind' and millions of years later nature still follows this principle of abundance. Nature produces more than is required. Look at plants and see the many flowers they produce, humans produce eggs and sperms in abundance! Here we see another universal law demontrated, the law of multiplication is part of our heritage as believers. God of more than enough knows no boundaries!

> 'You take care of the earth and water it, **making it rich and fertile**. The river of God has plenty of water; **it provides a bountiful harvest** of grain, for you have ordered it so' (Psalm 65:9 (NLT).

> 'You cause grass to grow for the livestock and plants for people to use. You allow them to produce food from the earth' Psalm 104:14 (NLT).

If right now you don't have what you desire, it's easy to ask, 'Where is this abundance you are talking about?' When we read the story of the children of Israel going through the wilderness, it's easy to have an attitude about how ungrateful they were. I guess we have the biased privilege of reading their full story from end to beginning!

The children of Israel must have had great faith to believe in something they had not experienced before. We have no idea what mental torture they endured, but it is evident in their behaviour that it wasn't easy. They were plagued with mourning, complaining, ungratefulness, scarcity thinking and there was always something else they felt they needed! They were never content and placed demand after demand for the whole duration of 40 years.

Not long after the crossing of the Red Sea where they celebrated, there seemed to be one calamity after another. Sadly, this is the way it goes, when you are in scarcity or complaining state of mind, you attract more of the same! Thoughts are like magnets, they will bring you more of the same so be mindful of those supposedly innocent thoughts flying in and out of your mind unmanned!

The best way to overcome this challenge is to assume a gratitude mindset. Be grateful at all times; focus on what you have, not what you don't have. Appreciate even the small things in life, even the air you breathe.

There is an old hymn we used to sing that illustrates the gratitude attitude, *'count your blessings, name them one by one, and it will surprise you what the Lord has done'*.

Apostle Paul put it this way to the believers in Thessalonica:

'Be thankful in all circumstances, for this is God's will for you who belong to Christ Jesus' **(1 Thessalonians 5:18 NLT).**

One of the ways to overcome a scarcity mindset is to take action towards what you desire. Everyday there will be many opportunities that come your way that supports abundance. They don't always announce themselves so do look out for them, especially if you are operating under the scarcity mindset. Adopt a positive mental attitude knowing that God wants you to have abundance in every area of your life and your eyes will become accustomed to noticing them.

God's storehouse has more than enough and we can never exhaust it. Imagine how many generations have come before us, and we are still able to produce enough for the ever-increasing population. I was reading somewhere that the current population is equivalent to all the humans from previous generations put together! Yet we can still feed ourselves comfortably if we share generously all round. There is enough pie to go round, so never compare or complain about what someone else has. There is plenty for everyone.

The old proverb that says 'bad company corrupts good character' has been proven to be true. You become the company you keep, so choose carefully whom you walk with. If your company questions God's abundance and blames Him for poverty in the world, then be warned for you will find yourself doing the same!

> *"Stop being deceived: 'Wicked friends lead to evil ends'"* (1 Corinthians 15:33 ISV).

God has provided more than enough for all of us; we humans need to be responsible! Christ Jesus became poor so we could be rich and live abundant lives!

> *'You know the **generous grace** of our Lord Jesus Christ. Though **he was rich**, yet for your sakes he became poor, so that by his poverty **he could make you rich**'* (2 Corinthians 8:9 NLT).

Judgment or Forgiveness

> *'God saved you by his grace when you believed. And you can't take credit for this; it is a gift from God'* (Ephesians 2:8).

Judgment is something we pass out on a daily basis on others, and sadly most of it is based on assumption! We meet people; look at the way they dress, speak, their size, race and many more and make a judgment about them. We don't take the time to get to know them before we make that all-important decision. From then on, the person will be viewed with those lens in all that they do and say.

In the early days of my faith, I suppose I judged people based on whether they were a believer or not as that was what was taught! On reflection, this is shocking and a narrow view of who God is and contrary to the teaching of Christ Jesus! Sadly, I was not alone and this type of teaching still exists today.

Grace and maturity in my faith have brought me to a new level of understanding and the true depth of grace.

According to scripture, I can't take credit for my relationship with God; He reached out to me with His unconditional love! No, I didn't find God; He found me, but I ignored Him for a long time because He didn't fit my small worldview.

> *'But God proves His love for us in this: While we were still sinners, Christ died for us'* **(Romans 5:8 BSB).**

Our human judges in our courts operate under the framework of the justice system that sets laws of the land. Grace hardly features in sentences passed, though leniency may be shown for first-time offenders and in other unique circumstances. This is Apostle Paul's take on the effects of the law:

> *"What then shall we say? Is the Law sin? By no means! Indeed, I would not have been mindful of sin if not for the Law. For I would not have been aware of coveting if the Law had not said, 'Do not covet.'*
> *But sin, seizing its opportunity through the commandment, produced in me every kind of covetous desire. For apart from the Law, sin is dead. Once I was alive apart from the Law; but when the commandment came, sin sprang to life and I died.*
> *So I discovered that the very commandment that was meant to bring life actually brought death"*
> **(Romans 7:7-10 BSB).**

Everything produces after its own kind and while we are grateful for the law, judgment only bears fruit according to itself and statistics show that some people do end up becoming hardened criminals after being jailed just once!

Forgiveness, on the other hand, bears a different kind of fruit. Once pardoned, there is a seed of forgiveness that is sowed in that person's heart. That person has been shown undeserved favour; a seed has been sown, and in time it will produce after its own kind.

God does not forgive us because we are good; even with the greatest good we could ever master, we have no ability to match His standard of good! He knows this, so He extends an undeserved gift called grace.

Our job is to receive this precious gift. Most of us struggle with this concept as it is unfamiliar and contrary to what we are taught that we have to earn everything we have. Nothing is free we are told.

We have the freedom to choose; regardless of what you've been taught, do not allow fear of judgment to rob you of what is rightfully yours!

> *'For God has not given us a spirit of fear and timidity, but of power, love, and self-discipline'* **(2 Timothy 1:7 NLT).**

God wants you to experience the fullness of joy, live under grace and comfortably walk in the fullness of what He has prepared for you.

> *'No power in the sky above or in the earth below - indeed, nothing in all creation will ever be able to separate us from the love of God that is revealed in Christ Jesus our Lord'* **(Romans 8:39 NLT).**

CHAPTER 8

ASK, SEEK, KNOCK AND IT IS GIVEN

Keep on asking, and you will receive what you ask for. Keep on seeking, and you will find. Keep on knocking, and the door will be opened to you. —
Matthew 7:7 (NLT)

Ask

Asking here is more than a dictionary definition. It is loaded with deeper spiritual meaning. From this perspective, there are many ways of asking. The attitude by which you ask for something will be the first determinant of the response you get. There is also knowing your right in asking – if you know something is yours, there is little or no contemplation; it's more about taking what belongs to you.

Many times in prayer we are not asking; we are begging, and in that attitude, we really have low expectancy to receive.

'You want what you don't have, so you scheme and kill to get it. You are jealous of what others have, but you can't get it, so you fight and wage war to take it away from them. **Yet you don't have what you want because you don't ask God for it. And even when you ask, you don't get it because your motives are all wrong** - *you want only what will give you pleasure'* **(James 4:2-3 NLT).**

Reading from what Jesus said in Matthew 7:7 and what Apostle James said in the text above, there are three things which are key to asking:

1. Persistence – you must keep on asking.
2. Motive/Intention– why do you want it?
3. Right to ask – He is your Father.

I've heard many begging and unsure prayers and I used to pray them too! Frustration and uncertainty that comes with not knowing what God is saying ends up killing the faith! Today most people lack persistence and give up very quickly especially in today's 'instant' culture where things happen 'now' – from microwave food to instant messaging!

Even parents want their children to do well and excel in life without taking exams, which build the resilience to persist, a key requirement to successful living.

We are used to demanding what we want, whether it's good for us or not; the attitude that says, I must have it because I want it or so and so has it! The Bible reminds us that a good father will only give their child those gifts he believes are right and appropriate for the child. If earthly fathers know how to do this, how much more our heavenly Father!

There are many times when I look back at my prayers and I thank God He didn't answer all of them! Why? My asking was foolish and self-seeking, lacking the right motive yet at the time of asking I thought I desperately needed the result!

One of the keys to asking is having **clarity** in what you are asking for. Shopping in today's digital world is different from the traditional manned shops when you had to ask the shopkeeper for what you wanted.

Imagine going to the shop to buy sweets and saying to the shopkeeper you would like to buy sweets. With so many varieties of sweets available, if you are not specific you could end up with nothing or whatever the shopkeeper likes. The honour is on you to be as specific as possible, remove all ambiguity and give the shopkeeper the right description of what you want. If you don't do the latter, you can't blame the shopkeeper for giving you the wrong sweets. You can be as angry as you want but it's really down to you what you get. James points this fact out to us when he writes this; *'because ye ask amiss!'* **(James 4:3)**.

Let's not ask wrongly or amiss as James put it; remember it's up to you to be as clear as possible about what you want and in great detail so that when you see it, you will recognise it straight away!

I used to have a laugh with one of my colleagues at work who coined the phrase 'food envy' before it was popular. We would go to restaurants together and order food separately. At the end, he would always want to have what was on my plate saying, 'I didn't order that' in reference to his food.

While food envy is laughable, we are not different in our asking. We even say, 'we don't always get what we want' and are happy to accept that! This kind of attitude creates wrong expectations and remember;

thinking or dwelling on something in your mind is a form of prayer!

Be sure you know what you want when you go to God in prayer; He is the giver of every good gift, and He's telling us to ask and to keep on asking. His storehouse has unlimited supply that never run dry.

The other challenge to receiving is that people don't even ask; they talk themselves out of receiving even before they start! They don't feel worthy of what they desire because they don't think they are good enough! I've had many conversations where I've asked, 'How do you know it's not possible?' What I get is reasons and excuses but nothing backed by any evidence from the word of God. God does not see you the way you see yourself; don't allow lies from the enemy to deny you of God's favour and blessing that is rightfully yours.

Generally, we only expect one answer from God every time we pray, that's a resounding YES regardless of the prayer. This is not accurate and it causes a lot of pain, dissapointment and misunderstaning among believers. We are left confused wondering why God answers some prayers and not others. I would like to bring to your attention the three types of answer you should expect and accept when you pray, each one of them as valid as the other two:

a) No
b) Wait
c) YES

Whichever one of the answers you get, it is given for your good with love and knowledge of your past, present and future. I mentioned earlier of my gratitude for unanswered prayers, the 'NO' didn't feel good at the time but now it makes sense!

'Such love has no fear, because perfect love expels all fear. If we are afraid, it is for fear of punishment, and this shows that we have not fully experienced his perfect love' (1 John 4:18 NLT)

Negativity

Finally, brothers and sisters, whatever is true, whatever is noble, whatever is right, whatever is pure, whatever is lovely, whatever is admirable – if anything is excellent or praiseworthy – think about such things. – Philippians 4:8

There are Bible texts that transmit peace purely by reading them; they are simple in their construction. The text above from the book of Philippians is one of those. What would happen if we all follow the instructions of Apostle Paul to the church in Philippi in what we do every day?

What most people don't realise is that they are their own enemy! There is no diplomatic way of stating that, it is what it is.

> *'You are snared with the words of your mouth, you are taken with the words of your mouth'* **(Proverbs 6:2 KJ2000B).**

Apostle Paul gives us the remedy, the cure to this damaging self-trap. We need to focus on the things that are positive about us and around us. The words we use in our prayer can be so mixed up emotionally; positive and negative language at the same time that you end up undoing the same prayers you've been offering to God.

Ask yourself, what is praiseworthy and good that you can see around you? Take the time and speak it out to God in gratitude and appreciation. This is more powerful than rehearsed words from a prayer book or your head!

You can test your heart attitude by checking in with yourself. For example, what do you say when you see a lovely affluent neighbourhood, a nice car on the road, luxury or things that signify wealth? Do you sneer, make a negative comment or do you appreciate how wonderfully blessed they are and imagine how it would feel to be in their position?

Your automatic reaction comes from your subconscious with so much emotion and feeling which in itself is a powerful prayer than you realise!

Apostle Paul says that we should *'pray constantly'* **(I Thessalonians 5:17)** and we surely do however, most people do not realise that their inner dialogue is prayer too!

Negativity is toxic, poisonous and will destroy any person regardless of their level of spirituality. It is more powerful and effective than the physical environment where you live or work. Your true nature is who you are when no one is watching you. The comments you make, the unspoken responses, thoughts that run through your mind create your reality! Death is hardly instant, most things that cause either spiritual or physical death are gradual; they happen over a long period of time.

Every conversation we have has the potential to be life giving or otherwise; we must therefore be mindful not just about what we say but what we are hearing!

For many years I've been working on my 'attitude' – who I am when I am alone. While people can be fooled, God can't! He knows what I'm going to say even before I open my mouth. I need to continuously check my 'attitude gauge' with those that live with me. When there is no crowd cheering and the stage lights are off, who am I?

Negativity is so powerful and getting out of its stronghold requires conscious effort. It starts with identifying the underlying habits in thoughts and speech. Ralph Waldo Emerson[viii] borrowing from the book of Proverbs said, *'A man is what he thinks about all day long'*.

What are you filling your mind with?

> ***'For as he thinks within himself, so he is**. He says to you, 'Eat and drink!' But his heart is not with you'* **(Proverbs 23:7 NASB).**

Spiritual Persona

> *'Don't be misled, you cannot mock the justice of God. You will always harvest what you plant'* **(Galatians 6:7 (NLT).**

There was once a popular TV programme in U.K. called *'You are what you eat'* and while the truth about that title could be argued, I know spiritually I am what I eat! What about you? Have you found this to be true?

Is there a correlation between what you read, listen and say to how you feel? For many years I didn't realise that I was a spiritual being first and foremost! Whilst I believed the Bible and what it says about me, I didn't quite know what part of me it was referring to.

I didn't know who I was. As shocking as this might sound, I had missed this profound truth that the Bible is never speaking to the physical me but *spiritual* me! The Bible says that you and I are *made in the image and likeness of God*; this does not refer to our physical person but the spirit!

This truth however was transformational and while even today I still can't comprehend the fullness of my spiritual persona, I revel in knowing that I am more than what meets the eye. I want to experience God's perfect will for my life on earth exactly as the blueprint in heaven:

'Your kingdom come, Your will be done, **on earth as it is in heaven'** (Matthew 6:10 BSB)

Another text that addresses our spirit persona is in 1 Corinthians 3. Again, Apostle Paul is not talking about the physical me but my spirit self.

The message of the Bible is all about the spiritual man, God's temple where His Spirit dwells. You are more spiritual than you realise; you were designed that way so you can commune with God.

> *'Do you not know that you yourselves are God's temple, and that God's Spirit dwells in you?'* **(1 Corinthians 3:16 BSB).**

What we feed on spiritually should be of great concern for our spiritual muscle is born of that. If you observe body builders, you will see how specific they are about their eating regiment and what they eat. If they don't follow this regiment they can't build muscle and we should adapt the same attitude if we want to build spiritual muscle.

The spirit man is always at work, going up and down to God to deliver your requests in form of your words and thoughts! Let me repeat this verse here:

> *'You are snared with the words of your mouth, you are taken with the words of your mouth'* **(Proverbs 6:2 KJ2000B).**

God has set laws in the universe, and they work, whether one believes in them or not. We reap a spiritual harvest of our planting whether we understand the law of seedtime and harvest or not!

It is law that you cannot plant an apple seed and get an orange tree, and equally, an orange tree will not give you apples. These are spiritual laws manifested physically, everything produces after its own kind.

We must understand what we want first then plant the chosen seed not vice versa. This may sound very simplistic but it's fundamental to understanding the things that come to us in life. We are fully responsible though not necessarily conscious of it! This is what causes a lot of pain and confusion but if you trace your thoughts backwards, you will see origins of events in your life.

Precious metals are never found anyhow on the streets, they are mined deep in the earth and there are specialised techniques and processes. This requires discipline, persistence, investment with many challenges and struggles before success.

Faith walk is the same; if you want to have those spiritual muscles then you must be prepared to put in the work! It is attainable, there are many before us who persevered even through persecution to set great examples. Take time and read Hebrews 11 for references.

I have mentioned and quoted many of these faith successes in this book but there are many more even in our modern times that we read about. In my early days as a believer, I read many biographies, they inspired and challenged me to be more than just a Sunday morning believer! I always wondered how they kept going and not give up. How could they have been encouraged?

> *'Not that I have already obtained all this, or have already arrived at my goal, but **I press on** to take hold of that for which Christ Jesus took hold of me'*
> **(Philippians 3:12 NIV).**

Remember, your mind is wonderful and like a healthy, fertile intricate garden, it will grow every thought seed that is planted in it! You just need to sow it.

Press On

Christ Jesus taught profound life lessons through telling stories referred to as parables in the Bible. Jesus didn't always give the interpretation of His stories, but in the story below taken from the book of Luke He did give an interpretation. He wanted to make sure this important message of 'pressing on' was not lost. I have included the full text below for completeness.

'Then Jesus told his disciples a parable to show them that they should always pray and not give up. He said: 'In a certain town there was a judge who neither feared God nor cared what people thought. And there was a widow in that town who kept coming to him with the plea, 'Grant me justice against my adversary.'
For some time he refused. But finally he said to himself, 'Even though I don't fear God or care what people think, yet because this widow keeps bothering me, I will see that she gets justice, so that she won't eventually come and attack me!'
And the Lord said, 'Listen to what the unjust judge says. And will not God bring about justice for his chosen ones, who cry out to him day and night? Will he keep putting them off? I tell you, he will see that they get justice, and quickly. However, when the Son of Man comes, will he find faith on the earth'" **(Luke 18: 1-8 NIV).**

I don't know how many times you have prayed concerning your financial status, but I know how disheartening it can be when nothing seems to be happening! I know too well how it feels because I have been there many times. In human terms, the will to give up is always greater than the desire to continue in faith!

As I ponder on this, I am reminded of Daniel when he prayed and the 21 days of waiting it took to get an answer to him which we think is a long time and compare our waiting to his. In my personal prayer life, there are times I have waited for years before the answer came.

Looking at the text above, what can we learn from this unnamed woman Christ Jesus was talking about? Simply, keep on pressing on without looking at time as the determinant. The judge had more power and authority than the woman, yet in the end it's her persistence that wore him down.

'God is never early or late', this statement is easier said than actively believed. We generally hear it from people trying to be encouraging. The Teacher writing in the book of Ecclesiastes says there is a time for everything under the sun! When I was given the word that I would have a son, like Hannah, I was excited and danced for joy but it took 8 years before it was fulfilled!

'Why so long?' I asked. I still don't know why and it's now immaterial as the gift makes the waiting worthwhile! What I can affirm is this: in that period of waiting, there were spiritual mountains to climb, valleys to cross, storms and deserts to overcome and it didn't seem like it was ever going to be possible.

The words in the book of Isaiah 40:31 kept me going:

'But those who trust in the LORD will find new strength. They will soar high on wings like eagles. They will run and not grow weary. They will walk and not faint' **(Isaiah 40:31 NLT).**

Surely, at times it would get so dark but hope would rise like the early morning sun and faith would be awakened, revived and refocused on the prophetic word. Many die spiritually in the time of waiting, we must know and understand this in order to have the right survival tools! If you are going to keep on believing that He who promised is faithful, you need to be on the right mental attitude even when the answer seems like it will never come.

Learn to encourage yourself in the Lord, in your secret place when you are alone and the spirit of discouragement stalks to kill you. Jesus overcame the devil by the words from the book of Isaiah; learn to love the word of God and use it as weapon to victory!

You and I will overcome by the word of our testimony; it is our sword and shield and you must never be shy to use it in your life circumstances! I quote the word of God unreservedly to myself and to the circumstances that face me more than I will ever quote it to others. This is necessary on two fronts, as a reminder to me and for the circumstance to know what I confidently believe in.

I must also point this out to you: the spirit of discouragement and quitting is relentless and tests us all, so keep watch. This spirit is a master at sowing seeds of doubt, the original question the 'serpent' asked Eve, *'did he really say that...'* will come to you over and over and you must learn to identify it and silence it!

Trauma to Transformation

As I come to the end of this book, I am delighted that I have been able to share some of what the Lord has laid on my heart yet burdened because I know there is more to share on this subject.

Over the last 20 years, I have seen God move in miraculous ways in my life; way beyond what I could have asked or imagined. I have experienced many seasons in my life, yet in them all, God has been faithful!

When God raised me from my deathbed, neither my family nor friends really understood why it had happened! I was like Lazarus with an unknown mission; my trauma had birthed a new beginning, a transformation and confirmed my calling!

I've been on an incredibly challenging yet fulfilling journey. I'm an overly optimistic person full of faith especially as I see God at work every step of the way, involved in the intricate matters of my life. In nature, no precious metal is formed overnight and it's not easy to mine either.

I'm so blessed to be a covenant child, I hang onto every word that He speaks to me or through me.

*'For I am confident of this, that He who began a good work in **me** will continue to perfect it until the day of Christ Jesus'* **(Philippians 1:6 BSB)**.

I expect the supernatural in my life; I will not settle for anything else!

FINAL WORDS

In this book I have shared wealth principles and listed the scriptures that go with them; now it's left for you to take hold of them and run with them. Like Habbakuk advices *(Habbakuk 2:2)*, write your wealth vision and make it clear and finally, run with it. He has already provided for you!

It amazes me when I see the privilege God has availed me, travelling to countries like Albania, Holland, Slovenia, U.S.A, Canada, Nigeria, India, United Emirates, Tanzania, Hong Kong, South Africa and more sharing His love and what he desires for each one of us. He is personal and knows you intimately.

I pray that the words and the spirit of this book will accomplish that which they were sent to do!

There is more to come, send me an email today serah@serahlister.com

*'**But I press on** toward the goal for the prize of the upward call of God in Christ Jesus' (Philippians 3:14).*

BONUS CONTENT

FAITH – THE EDGE OF BELIEVE!

The truth in the words written in Ezekiel 16 are shocking yet so real to me, I was despised and abandoned the day I was born and a stranger passed by, saw me and picked me up! This man went to the room where all the nursing mothers were with their babies and asked, *'Whose baby is this?'*

This same stranger was there before the foundations of the earth; He knew my form and the very day I would appear on earth! He made sure I lived so the covenant would be fulfilled. I don't remember him but I know who rescued me on the fateful day and said, 'Live'!

"On the day you were born your cord was not cut, nor were you washed with water to make you clean, nor were you rubbed with salt or wrapped in cloths. No one looked on you with pity or had compassion enough to do any of these things for you. Rather, you were thrown out into the open field, ***for on the day you were born you were despised.***

> ***Then I passed by and saw you** kicking about in your blood, and as you lay there in your blood I said to you, 'Live!'"* **(Ezekiel 16: 4-6 NIV).**

The events of the day were hidden from me and rejection continued into my adult life but whilst I didn't consciously understand, my soul knew what had happened.

As an adult, I started working with rejected children in the slums and streets of Nairobi; my Sunday base had over 500 kids hungry for God's love and acceptance. It gave me such pleasure to see them being transformed by His love, so I spent time and the money I had on this wonderful mission. Little did I know I was reaching out to heal the child inside me who still wanted to be accepted!

Then God called me to England and a new exciting phase of my life started.

My call to England didn't have a 'when' so I carried on doing what I was doing and waited for the green light. Instead of a green light, a deep darkness seemed to come and overtake my life. Suddenly, I found myself lying in a hospital bed, skin and bone was what was left of me and the doctor concluded I was to die within 7 days! I was 28 years old, too young to die!

What about this call to England?

When I looked at my circumstances, I really had little reason I could give to have my life spared. I had no children, no dependents, and my family could survive without my financial support. That part of my case was quite obvious to me.

The look of fear or imminent death was evident on the faces of those that came to see me, not to mention even I was scared of what I saw of myself - I didn't recognise me.

I had nothing to lose, so I decided to have a deep heart-to-heart conversation with God. He says in Isaiah 1:18, *'Come let us reason together,'* and so I thought, this was my one chance!

(Book coming soon...)

This is an excerpt from my upcoming book with the same title as this section; do look out for it. If you would like to pre-order send an email to serah@serahlister.com

I'm also available for speaking engagements, I speak on faith and teach others how to use and

manifest FAITH as a God-given tool to live a fulfilled life. I also demonstrate faith using examples from my own life journey.

The traumas and trials you have been through are not meant to crush you; they are meant to work to *transform* you.

You are a pearl of great price!

'20 BEAUTIFUL WOMEN – AFRICA EDITION'
(Amazon Best Seller)

The Blessed Goat

As I stood in front of 120 girls who were graduating from our IT boot camp for women in Tanzania, I realised they were looking up to me like I was a goddess who had come down from above to help them. Something happened in me, and I realised they had to know my true story. They had no idea of my humble beginnings, and I owed it to them if I was truly going to make a difference in their lives. I didn't want to be another perfect role model looking sharp and successful like I'd never struggled a day in my life. My images on social media were polished and didn't tell that story – the story that changed my life forever.

I was born in a little village on the slopes of Mount Kenya. It's the most beautiful place in the world to me; from the vantage point on the slopes as you look across the plains far in the horizon, you see the Aberdare Ranges spanning the full breadth of the horizon. In the summer, the plains are a beautiful purple and the only other place I see such beautiful purple in nature is the now protected Bluebell Fields in England. The Jacaranda trees bring welcomed contrast in this evergreen paradise. I wish I could say my childhood was the same, but it was far from it.

I was in primary school and things had changed in my family. The house girl and the farm boy had left and we (the children) had to do everything. The little princess had lost her title and she had chores to do. The cows were waiting to be milked before and after school. Oh, and the goats and sheep had to be taken to their pasture and tied to the pole for the day so they didn't get into the neighbour's garden. For me, the worst of the chores was the goat. Oh, the blessed goat – the woe of my life! The tears...the hatred – all in one morning!

Almost all the married women I knew had farms and farm animals. That was their existence – daily, weekly, and all year round even on Sundays. The farm animals had to be taken care of... There was no day off on a farm.

When my elder sister got married young and had her first child, her father-in-law who was a traditionalist insisted that they had to pay a dowry. The old man was adamant that he had to pay the traditional way, no substitutes. He brought goats, sheep, cows, and all the other trimmings with pomp song and dance. I was very young and watched the whole affair from a distance; it was my first experience of such.

When the party was over, we were left with goats we didn't eat – wild goats in my opinion. To be honest, I don't remember what else was left besides what became mine. It had a white coat; therefore, we fondly named it Keru. It was mine to take care of.

Writing this takes me back to my father's nine acres of land on the slopes. Every morning I would hear my mother calling me to get up for school. It wasn't really for school; it was to do the chores before school...while she slept. I've never been a morning person and I hated getting up, let alone doing all the chores. I was as skinny as a rake, and I remember my brothers teasing me by telling me that I should put some rocks in my pocket so I didn't get blown away by the wind. But, that didn't get me any sympathy. What needed to be done had to be done. Some days it would make me late for school, and I would get the cane because of it.

Get the e-book: serah@serahlister.com

To God be the glory!

END NOTES

[i] The Lord Who Provides (Genesis 22:14)

[ii] The Lord That Heals (Exodus 15:26)

[iii] An edible substance that, according to the **Bible** God provided for the **Israelites** during their travels in the desert

[vi] Melchizedek, the King of Salem

[v] Gerard Hendrik Hofstede - *a Dutch social psychologist and Professor Emeritus of Organizational Anthropology and International Management at Maastricht University in the Netherlands*

[vi] In Christianity the third person of the Trinity

[vii] Stephen Covey, *The 7 Habits of Highly Effective People*, 1990

[viii] Ralph Waldo Emerson - *(May 25, 1803 – April 27, 1882)*

REFERENCES

Scripture quotations are taken from the following sources:

Holy Bible, New Living Translation (NLT), copyright ©1996, 2004, 2007.
Used by permission of Tyndale House Publishers, Inc., Carol Stream, Illinois 60188.
All Rights Reserved.

Holy Bible, New International Version®, NIV®
Copyright © 1973, 1978, 1984, 2011 by Biblica, Inc.®

Used by permission. All rights reserved worldwide.

Berean Study Bible (BSB)
© 2016 by Bible Hub and Berean.Bible
Used by Permission. All rights Reserved.

Holman Christian Standard Bible®, (HCSB)
Copyright © 1999, 2000, 2002, 2003, 2009 by Holman Bible Publishers.
Used by permission.

New American Standard Bible Copyright © (NASB) 1960, 1962, 1963, 1968, 1971, 1972, 1973, 1975, 1977, 1995 by The Lockman Foundation, La Habra, Calif. All rights reserved.

Scripture taken from the New King James Version® (NKJV). Copyright © 1982 by Thomas Nelson. Used by permission. All rights reserved.

King James Bible

The Holy Bible: *International Standard Version®* (ISV) Release 2.1
Copyright © 1996-2012 The ISV Foundation
ALL RIGHTS RESERVED INTERNATIONALLY.

The ESV® Bible (The Holy Bible, English Standard Version®) copyright © 2001 by Crossway Bibles, a publishing ministry of Good News Publishers. The ESV® text has been reproduced in cooperation with and by permission of Good News Publishers. Unauthorized reproduction of this publication is prohibited. All rights reserved.

Webster Bible Translation

GOD'S WORD® is a copyrighted work of God's Word to the Nations. Quotations are used by permission. Copyright 1995 by God's Word to the Nations. All rights reserved.

The Names of God Bible (without notes) © 2011 by Baker Publishing Group. (NOG - GW)

Scripture is taken from GOD'S WORD®, © 1995 God's Word to the Nations. Used by permission of Baker Publishing Group.

Serah Lister

The Original Aramaic New Testament in Plain English- with Psalms & Proverbs

Copyright © 2007; 8th edition Copyright © 2013

All rights reserved. Used by Permission.

International Children's Bible®
Copyright© 2015 by Tommy Nelson, a division of Thomas Nelson, Inc.

The American King James Version (AKJV) is Produced by Stone Engelbrite. It is a simple word for word update from the King James English. Care was taken to change nothing doctrinally, but to simply update the spelling and vocabulary. Grammar has not been changed. manner you wish: copy it, sell it, modify it, etc. You may not copyright it or prevent others from using it. You may not claim that you created it, because you didn't.

"Scripture quotations taken from the *Amplified® Bible (AMP)*,
Copyright © 2015 by The Lockman Foundation
Used by permission. www.Lockman.org"

The King James 2000 Bible, copyright © Doctor of Theology Robert A. Couric 2000, 2003 Used by permission. All rights reserved.

KIANJIRIGUA
PUBLISHING

www.ingramcontent.com/pod-product-compliance
Lightning Source LLC
Chambersburg PA
CBHW061647040426
42446CB00010B/1616